Dealing with Divas
and other
Difficult Personalities

A Mindful Approach to Improving
Relationships in Your
Business or Organization

Castle Mount
Media

Castle Mount
— Media —

CASTLE MOUNT MEDIA GMBH & CO KG
Burgbergstr. 94c
91054 Erlangen
Germany

Bibliographic information for the German National Library
can be found under http://dnb.d-nb.de

Printed in the United States of America and
for International Distribution in the United Kingdom

Book design by Susan Veach
Cover Illustration by Elke Schmalfeld

ISBN 978-3-9818472-1-5 (Paperback)
ISBN 978-3-9818472-2-2 (eBook)

Table of Contents

To Norbert, Stephanie, and Benjamin
for your love, inspiration,
and fantastic sense of humor
Every day has been a wonderful adventure!

ACKNOWLEDGEMENTS

Writing a book can be one of the most rewarding and daunting experiences, and for me at least, there is no way that I would have been able to do this on my own.

First and foremost, I would like to thank all of my clients and seminar participants over the years who have allowed me to have a glance into their lives. For their trust and willingness to share, I am truly grateful.

Also, for friends, colleagues and teachers both in the operatic world and in the training world, thank you for sharing your ideas about this subject. It is amazing how many parallels there are between the operatic world and business, especially when it comes to divas! Larger than life personalities, insecurities, and the need for recognition are as present in business as they are in theater; they are just a little more subtle. I am grateful for wonderful new insights into these parallels!

There are several people without whom I can definitively say I would not have been able to finish this book. First, my book coach and slave driver Les Kletke. At the top of my manuscript were engraved the words: "Les has NO tolerance for not writing!" Without his patience and encouragement (and very clear views on the nonexistence of "writers' block"!), I think I would have long since given up. Thank you, Les!

Also, I would not have been able to make it through the last stretch of this without a dear friend and colleague of mine from my Duke days, Suzanne Purtee. Suzanne has the unique combination of understanding both the music world and running organizations. Her input has been absolutely invaluable.

I believe that success comes by surrounding yourself with networks that support you. These networks should be measured not only by the interactions of its members but also by how much they force us to grow personally and professionally. The following networks have helped me grow personally and professionally, and through them, I have become a better person and performance coach for it.

One of my greatest honors is be associated with the Evolutionary Business Council, an organization of thought leaders, authors, and speakers, who are dedicated to changing the world for the better. Its founder, bestselling author Teresa de Groisbois, together with Pam Bayne, have supported me in this remarkable journey in so many ways, I can't even begin to list them here. Thank you both for sharing your knowledge and experience, for keeping me on track, and for helping me build up a wonderful network of thought leaders, so that we can reach and help as many people as possible. You are truly an inspiration to all who come in contact with you!

Another integral organization to my development in business and networking is the Business Network International. I would like to thank our Executive Directors Wolfgang Thoma, Ina Heinl, and Armin Lediger for their trust and support, and I would like to shout out a thank you to Bacchus, Kerner, and the Team of Directors led by Harald Lais, Michael Mayer, and Danja Hermethschweiler. My thanks to Gunther Verleger, Ivan Misner, and Graham Weihmiller for their tips and advice during the production of this book. The opportunity to be a part of the Author Mentoring Group led by Ivan Misner was inspiring. Thank you!

It is not possible to mention all of the people who have helped me in this process through encouraging words, an exchange of ideas, sharing of experiences, or actually reading through different drafts of this book. I would like to thank my Mastermind Group with Gudrun Reinschmidt, Daniela Borschel, Monika Ladwein, Ulrike Horky, and Claudia Sigel. I would also like to thank the Ladies Who Read (a lot more than I do!): Marly Schaule, Wendy Ran, Karen Christenson, and Jen Lauterbach. For encouragement and support in ways unimaginable, I would like to thank Robert Dilts, the late Dan Poynter, Leslie Carroll, Herbert Guggenheim, George Gopen, Margit Hertlein, Martin Limbeck, Lothar Seiwert, Renee Moore, Audry Wagner-Morales, Stephen McGahee, Margaret Beier, and my late parents, Jane and Edge McGahee.

For their many insights and for introducing me to the Biostructure-Analysis, my deepest thanks go to Evelyn Wild, Norbert Milde and the late Juergen Schoemen.

To my organisational team, thank you to Marivic Aurea, Lana Santa Marie, and Marife Gaspar.

Last but not least, I would like to thank my family. It is not easy coming home to a person who seems to spend hours on the computer talking about deadlines or asking about syntax. Norbert, Stephanie, and Benjamin, you are my inspiration and strength. Your patience, sense of humor, and ability to keep me grounded are what keeps me going. With my deepest love, thank you.

Laura Baxter
April 2017

INTRODUCTION

Over the course of writing this book, so many people have shared their own personal stories with me and asked questions about how they can improve relationships with those difficult people in their lives. Many have confessed that don't want to improve the relationship; they don't want to have anything to do with their "diva." Some just laugh and say, "Good luck with that!"

Many of the stories have been heart-wrenching and sad. Strong relationships which have turned sour. Friendships or partnerships that have abruptly ended due to some misunderstanding or perceived difference. I have spoken with people who have been carrying a grudge for years and don't know how to let go of it. I have spoken with people who have so much stress caused by poor relationships at work that they literally become nauseated as they enter the door of their office building.

In the many discussions and questions about my work on this book, there is one question that has *never* come up: "*Why are you writing about this topic?*" Thus far, no one has said that this topic is not relevant or that we already have too many books on this subject.

The most common question that I have gotten from almost everyone, even if they don't have a major conflict with someone in their lives, is "*When will it be coming out?*"

The interest in this topic seems overwhelming. I am grateful and very humbled by the responses that I thus far received. For the resonance that *Dealing with Divas* seems to be generating and for the many people who have shared their stories and helped me on this journey, I am deeply grateful.

MY STORY

Perhaps before I go into more details about why I wrote this book, I should tell you a little bit about my personal history and how I came to write this book.

In so very many ways my life has been blessed. As a young singer in my late twenties, I could look back at many successes. As an undergraduate at Emory University, I was the first recipient of the Louis Sudler Award for the Arts, and during my graduate studies at The

Ohio State University, I was given opportunities and support in so many ways, from teaching classes from between 40 and 120 students to participating in research to furthering my understanding of music repertoire and how the voice functions.

After that time, I had the honor of being on the faculty at Duke University and later, touring with the National Opera Company, an experience that allowed me to sing leading roles many, many times for many different audiences. During this time I got to sing on various regional opera stages, and I was asked to be the singing voice of Serena Joy (played by Faye Dunaway) in the feature film The Handmaid's Tale. Also during this time, I met the man who was later to become my husband while he was doing an internship at Duke.

In the American opera scene, it is expected that American opera singers spend at least some time, usually several years, in Europe singing, learning about different European cultures, and studying the languages. It makes the interpretation of the operas we perform, especially those sung in foreign languages, easier and more authentic.

For me, for a variety of reasons, I knew that I would be going to Germany. German was not, by far, my best foreign language, nor was the German operatic repertoire my main repertoire, but I sensed that the place I needed to be at that point in my life was Germany.

This background is important to understand how I got to where I am today. It is important, because it explains what happened when I hit rock bottom.

I was in a foreign country doing roughly 30-40 auditions over the course of three months, and I was not getting the results I needed. Everyone liked my voice, but it was shortly after the reunification of Germany. Because of budget cuts, theaters were being closed or were having to cut back on the number of singers they could employ. A lot of my repertoire could be handled by sopranos who were already on the payroll. In addition, for the first time since World War II, singers from Eastern Block countries were allowed to freely travel to Western Europe. They were less expensive and more exotic than yet another American singer.

I went from a situation where my career was on a steady upward trajectory, a situation where I had 4-5 performances per week and was asked to do wonderful repertoire with wonderful orchestras to a situation where I had absolutely no work. My savings were dwindling and, on top of it all, I found out that I was pregnant. I realized that I had to make some very serious decisions about my future, and it was very clear that it was not the future that I had imagined.

Several things were very clear to me: I wanted to have my baby, and I wanted to marry it's father. Other decisions were not quite so easy. The first decision was where we were to live. My husband offered to move to America with me if I wanted to go back, but I had not yet accomplished the things that I needed to accomplish in Europe. I decided to stay, even though it meant that my original plan of three to five years in Germany would now be extended indefinitely. And none of this changed the fact that I was still unemployed.

For me, music was my life. Everything that I had done to this point in my life was to understand how the voice works, how to master and interpret the most beautiful vocal repertoire, and to be the best actress I could be. I had been given the gift of time and means to pursue this dream, and now life was a lot more complicated.

The audition process had never been easy for me. On the stage I was great. Larger than life, exciting, a diva, if you will. At auditions, however, I tended to be very serious. More than once I heard from artistic directors that had they not seen me on stage before the audition, I probably would not have gotten a contract. Some auditions went very well, but they were always a challenge.

In Germany after my daughter's birth, I continued auditioning for agents and theaters. The audition process, which had never been easy for me, was now even more challenging. I found that I sabotaged auditions even when I had sung the role I was auditioning for hundreds of times. Although I did get work singing concerts and teaching voice and although I still got to sing opera through connections in the USA, I felt that I needed to look at what was holding me back in these auditions. I needed to understand the psychological side of performing.

FROM OPERA SINGER TO PERFORMANCE COACH

After the birth of our son and after I got a position on the faculty teaching voice and speech development at the Friedrich Alexander University Erlangen-Nuremberg, my husband and I attended a seminar taught by Toni Robbins. Through this seminar I learned about Neurolinguistic Programming (NLP), and I realized that this could be what I was looking for.

As soon as I got home, I immediately signed up for an NLP Practitioner course. I continued my trainings in this and many other methods, and today I am a certified Master Trainer of NLP, a Suggestopedia Practioner, and a Structogram® trainer. I continue to learn as much as I can in many areas, especially in the areas of systemic and integral thought, mindfulness, hypnotherapy and solution-focused therapy.

I have had the honor of working with and learning from great thought leaders like Robert Dilts, Stephen Gilligan, Matthias Varga von Kibed, Insa Sparrer, Gunther Schmidt, and the late Bernd Isert and Tom Best. I mean it from the bottom of my heart when I say that I have truly been blessed to know these people.

Through these certifications I began giving trainings and coachings in businesses and organizations. These trainings and coachings were predominantly with people in leadership positions who either wanted to improve their performance skills or wanted to master the psychological side of performing.

I have had the honor of working with top executives, with start-up CEOs, with politicians and chief officers. I have worked with doctors and lawyers, with teachers and leaders of NGOs. Probably one of the most interesting tasks that I have had to date was working with security guards in a large city here in Germany. Their chief officer brought me in to help them learn to remain calm, centered and focused when facing some of the most unimaginable situations possible.

The focus of my work is presence, developing both a strong inner presence as well as a strong outer presence. I help my clients master using their voice and body language so that they can own the room while inwardly they remain calm, centered, and focused. They learn to connect to their inner selves and to their value systems so that they can dynamically communicate their message to their audience in an authentic and congruent manner.

WHY THIS BOOK?

One of things that I noticed over the years is that, more than anything else, we are emotionally most influenced and affected by the other people around us. Our beliefs about these other people and our experiences with them often distract us from being centered and focused. For example, someone suffering from stage fright is most commonly concerned about what *other people* will think. They do not want to make a mistake in front of the *other people*.

In working with teams, I have noticed how strongly the interpersonal relationships affect how successful the team will be. Conflicts happen easily. They happen all the time. What counts is how you deal with those conflicts. Are they treated as challenges to be overcome as a team or are they swept under the carpet and dismissed as individual problems to be dealt with privately?

There are times when I have had the honor of working with entire teams. This makes the process of understanding conflicts easier. Most of the time, however, I only have one person or one group of people to work with. The other people involved in the conflict are not present. In these situations my job is to help my clients deal with the people causing them difficulties by helping them remain calm, centered, and focused and by helping them reach their goals.

This book is the result of this work.

A FEW NOTES ABOUT THE BOOK

Although all of the stories in this book are real, all of the names (with the exception of members of my family) are fictitious. In some cases for the sake of brevity, I have merged different stories or situations together.

Also, please note that the term "Diva" refers to a person with whom you are having difficulties. This person may be male or female. It might even be a group of people. For our "Divas" I have chosen the personal pronoun "they," both because it was too difficult to go back and forth between "he" and "she" and because I do not at any level wish to imply that a typical diva — despite the feminine ending to the word — is either male or female.

As you will discover in the course of reading this book, not all of us consider the same persons to be difficult. If you look at the fun illustration by Elke Schmalfeld on the cover of this book, you may consider the somewhat larger female in the middle to be the diva. On the other hand, you might find her to be rather normal. You might consider one of the other persons on the cover to be your definition of a diva. This is intentional.

When I sent this drawing to various friends for their feedback, I was fascinated by which persons they related to and which persons they found "annoying." This is true in life. We are not all the same. Those persons who may be annoying to us may not be annoying to someone else.

For the sake of flow, I have put all references and notes at the end of the book separated by chapters. If you are interested in learning more about any of the methods discussed in the book, please refer to these endnotes or contact us with your questions. We would love to hear from you!

My dream with this book is to help as many people as possible master living and working with those people they find difficult. If you find this book helpful, please go to Amazon and Goodreads and leave us a great review. This will help *Dealing with Divas* rise in the Amazon and Google rankings and therefore help other people find the book. I would greatly appreciate your help in doing this.

Most of all, I hope that this book helps you. I hope that in the course of reading this book, you will have some new insights that will help you be strong in your situation and help you better deal with your diva!

Laura Baxter
Erlangen, Germany
April 2017

GETTING STARTED:
ALL ABOUT DIVAS

Chapter 1

Why Should We Care about Divas?

Has anyone ever made you feel small or insignificant? Acted rude or unprofessional towards you or your colleagues? I will never forget one particular time when that happened to me — on the stage in front of everyone.

It is the opening night of *Merry Wives of Windsor*, and I am playing the role of Meg Page. The theater is packed with an audience of enthusiastic theater-goers, who are applauding wildly. Our performance is a success.

We've already done our individual bows, and we're getting in place for the final group bow. This is when the entire cast holds hands, walks up to the edge of the stage, and bows.

That's when she does it. My colleague, the soprano with whom I am working, does the unthinkable. She totally blocks my bow!

I am standing to her right, and she sticks her right arm in front of me so that her arm is blocking my body. In all of my experience on stage, no one has ever tried to do such a thing. Other cast members are on my right, so I have no room to move further in that direction. My left hand — the hand she is holding — is pushed across my body so that it is almost touching my right hand. There is no physical way that I can bow. I just stand there like an idiot in front of a fervent audience of about a thousand people.

I decide to be prepared for the next performance. The next night, as we walk down for the group bow, I brace myself and make sure that I have enough room. I stick my left arm way out so that there is no way she can block me again. I will not let her take my space and make me feel small again.

That's what divas do. They take our space and make us feel small. I never spoke to my colleague about what happened that night. I simply didn't trust her, and I decided never to work with her again.

> Divas take our space and make us feel small. They rob us of precious time and energy.

IN YOUR ORGANIZATION

So what does this situation have to do with your business or organization? Everything.

One of the main causes of employee disengagement or dissatisfaction in teams is poor communication. This can result from not feeling respected or valued by peers or supervisors or from personal conflicts with other members of the team. Often team members feel at the mercy of the "divas" around them.

One of the greatest challenges in businesses and organizations today is employee engagement. In a recent study conducted by Effectory International in 31 European countries, only 23.9% of employees are actively engaged and committed to their work. Although the numbers in the USA are somewhat better, the most recent Gallup Employee Engagement Report found that only 32% of American workers are actively engaged and committed employees. In a Gallup Poll from 2011-2012 surveying 180 million employees in 142 countries, the statistics are even grimmer. Gallup found that

13% of employees are **engaged**
63% of employees are **not engaged**
24% of employees are **actively disengaged**

This means that internationally only 13% of employees are actively engaged and interested in the success of their organization. Only 13% of employees feel as if they fit in, are appreciated, and can contribute to the success of the organization. 87% are either "not engaged," meaning indifferent to the success of the organization, or "actively disengaged" employees who actively work against the success of their organization. Understandably, data shows that 79% of businesses are seriously worried about employee engagement and retention, making it, after leadership, their largest concern.

Why does this interest us when talking about dealing with divas? One of the main causes of employee disengagement is poor communication within teams. This can result from not feeling respected or valued by peers or supervisors or from personal conflicts with other members of the team. Often employees feel at the mercy of the divas around them.

My experience with Jeff illustrates a typical example of this.

JEFF

Jeff, a young, enthusiastic project manager, came to me to be coached. He had several presentations that he needed to give, and my job was to make him fit for the challenge, to help him fine-tune his presentation so that he could sell his product internationally and become the next up-and-coming star of his company.

In talking about his project and what he wants to communicate, he lets out a very telling statement.

"Sometimes I feel like I'm the only normal person in the place. Most of my colleagues are good at what they do, but it's really hard to work with them."

"For example?" I ask.

He goes on to explain that he has seventeen employees under him on his team — there used to be nineteen, but he had to let two people go. One person was let go because she was needed on another project and one because he was creating havoc in the team.

The troublesome employee kept trying to control everything, to get the last word in, and when he felt like some member of the team did a poor job on some aspect of a project, he voiced that he thought that the person was incompetent and stupid.

"Often," Jeff continues, "I have wondered if there hadn't been a better way to deal with Herb. He was really very talented and I would have liked to have had his input on the project, but no one wanted him around."

Several months later Jeff calls me to ask if we can get together for a cup of coffee. There are several people on his team who are threatening to leave if he doesn't fire Stan. Just as with Herb, Jeff feels that Stan has a lot of talent, but he is annoying everyone on the team. Could there be any way to solve the situation?

DIFFICULT PERSONALITIES

Each one of us is unique, and, like it or not, each of us may seem somewhat "special" to others – and not necessarily in a positive sense. If it makes you feel better, yes, some personalities are more "special" than others. Some people manage to offend others simply by entering the room, and others seem to be peacemakers who never seem to get into conflict with anyone.

In the operatic world, stereotypically the most difficult personalities are the tenors. The stereotypical tenor is known to be desperately in need of special attention, and they are often the brunt of many singers' jokes. We can't, however, do the show without tenors, because they most commonly have the leading role in the production. It doesn't help to replace them if they are causing difficulties, because you're only replacing them with another tenor! You might as well learn to deal with the tenor who is already there — and, if you succeed, you will find it to be rewarding and beautiful.

Often it's the same in a business. I'm sure that there are people in your organization who are not as easy to deal with as others, but they have an important role to play. The costs of replacing them far exceed

> I'm sure that there are people in your organization who are not as easy to deal with as others, but they have an important role to play. The costs of replacing them far exceed the costs of learning to integrate them into the group.

"Think about the advantage of a place where talent wants to stay 25 years. Your turnovers lower, you don't have as many people you have to train every year, break in every year, you don't have as many mistakes. A seasoned workforce does a better job – and they cost you less money."

— *David Rodriguez,
  CHRO, Marriott*

Mindful approach simply means being mindfully, or consciously aware of what is going on around you. In our work together here, it means being mindfully aware in four areas: 1) being mindfully aware of the situations in which you encounter your diva, 2) being mindfully aware of yourself while encountering the diva, 3) being mindfully aware of the needs of the diva, including their personality structure and personal motivations, and 4) being mindfully aware of the tools available to help you connect with your diva.

the costs of learning to integrate them into the group. If you were to let them go, you would be missing the positive contributions that they might have made to the group, and both you and they would miss out on an opportunity to grow and to learn more about yourselves and others.

No matter how difficult some people can be, it is possible to get along at some level with most of them. All you have to do is understand a few basics about their needs and about how they think. In addition, it is necessary to better understand yourself and how you react to those "special" people in your life.

In this book you will learn to understand others better, so that when you are confronted with situations in which you have to deal with the divas or other difficult personalities in your life, you will remain calm, centered, and focused. You will be able to communicate with them in a way that is productive and rewarding.

WHAT IS A MINDFUL APPROACH?

Mindful approach simply means being mindfully, or consciously aware of what is going on around you. In our work together here, it means being mindfully aware in four areas: 1) being mindfully aware of the situations in which you encounter your diva, 2) being mindfully aware of yourself while encountering the diva, 3) being mindfully aware of the needs of the diva, including their personality structure and personal motivations, and 4) being mindfully aware of the tools available to help you connect with your diva.

As Jeff said after we worked together, "I didn't realize how much time and energy I was spending being a peacemaker, trying to hold our team together. It cost me hours and hours of time and money, and it robbed me of countless hours of sleep." By helping Jeff to be consciously aware of his situation in all four of the areas mentioned above, he was able to take control of the situation.

The goal of this book is to save you time, money and, above all, energy. At best, having to deal with difficult personalities is a distraction from your goals. At worst, having divas or other difficult personalities in your life can be destructive. They cause conflicts, discontentment, and disengagement. In either case, being able to deal with divas will give you the peace of mind that you deserve.

HOW THIS BOOK CAN HELP YOU

Jeff knows his success is totally dependent on his ability to bring his team together to complete their project without any further delay.

His success — how he would be viewed in the company, whether or not he would get the new projects he wanted, and whether or not he would be considered for promotion — depended on his ability to understand his team. It is critical to effectively communicate with them and help them communicate with each other.

This latter point seemed impossible.

"Most of the members of the team don't even talk to Stan now." Jeff tells me as we drink our coffee. "And Stan isn't helping matters either. He constantly makes new demands on the team, and more often than not, he criticizes me for my leadership skills."

It is clear to Jeff that something needs to happen to turn things around, and it needs to happen quickly.

The options available to Jeff are limited. He could demand that Stan himself changes. This option, however, seems highly unlikely. Each time he discusses Stan's behavior with Stan, Stan gets angry and defensive, and he blames the other team members for the tensions.

Another option is to talk to the team about getting along with Stan. Jeff has tried this with some success. Everyone on the team understands the importance of the project, and they have been willing to look the other way in order to make progress.

Now, however, the team has lost its patience. What can Jeff do?

WHAT WILL WE BE DOING?

In the course of this book we will look at different situations similar to Jeff's and with help from the DIVA model, we will go through the steps necessary to isolate and to improve the situation you are experiencing with your diva.

THE DIVA MODEL

D — DEFINING THE SITUATION

The first step is to define the situation in which the conflict with your diva occurs. You will determine your goals for this situation, and you will examine exactly how and when you encounter your diva. Both of these processes will give you clarity as to what is going on with your diva and help you to obtain the necessary emotional distance to analyze the situation.

I — YOUR INNER STRENGTH

After we have defined when you interact with your diva and what your desired outcome is, we will move to the next phase of

"No one can make you feel inferior without your consent."

— *Eleanor Roosevelt,*
This is My Story

First and foremost our goal here is to help you achieve the outcomes you desire within a working relationship with your diva, all the while being able to remain calm, centered, and focused.

this process: finding and maintaining a strong inner state. Here our job is two-fold: 1) to show you what causes you to emotionally react to your diva, and 2) to give you concrete tools which will help you remain calm, centered, and focused.

V — VALUING YOURSELF AND THE OTHER PERSON

The next step is to value both yourself and the other person. This happens when you understand more about yourself— what your needs and desires are — and when you understand more about the diva and their needs. You will learn what their interests are, how to motivate them, and how to build a bridge to them in order to reach your goals.

A – ASSOCIATING WITH THE DIVA

According to the Merriam-Webster Dictionary, to associate means "to bring together or into relationship in any of various intangible ways," "to join as a partner, friend, or companion." In this phase we will find ways to help you begin to build a bridge to — or relationship with — the challenging people in your life. This is NOT about becoming friends with the other person or even liking the other person. This step is about building a bridge to the other person so that your goals and desires may be accomplished.

Of course, there are situations in which you will meet strong resistance. There will even be situations where it is impossible to build a bridge to the other person. We will look at these situations as well.

First and foremost our goal here is to help you achieve the outcomes you desire within a working relationship with your diva, all the while being able to remain calm, centered, and focused. You will develop a mindful awareness of the situation and of your own reaction to the situation and all the people involved. You will master dealing with divas!

GETTING STARTED

For our work together, pick out one situation you would like to work on, where you want the relationship to improve. Take a moment to write down as much about this situation and the people involved as possible.

"The secret to getting ahead is getting started."

— Mark Twain, Author

_____

_____

_____

_____

_____

_____

"A journey of a thousand miles begins with a single step."

— Lao-tzu, Ancient Chinese philosopher and writer

_____

_____

_____

_____

_____

_____

_____

_____

_____

_____

_____

_____

Chapter 2

What is a Diva, and How Do We Begin?

The word diva comes from the ancient Italian word *divus*, or god-like, divine. The first known modern use of the word was in the late 19th century and referred to a great female opera singer or prima donna.

In the mid to late 20th century, the word's meaning was expanded to include larger-than-life personalities not only in the operatic world, but also from film, television and other entertainment industries. At this time it also began to be used as a derogatory term referring to a person who invades other people's space and makes them feel small.

It is interesting to note that until very recently (the 1990's) the term "diva" was always attributed to a person from the outside — both in the positive "larger than life" and "god-like" form and in the negative "egotistic" and "overbearing" sense. It was not a term that one said about one's self. Only recently with Annie Lennox from the Diva or Joan Rivers' diamond diva necklace do we have stars naming themselves "diva."

For the purposes of this book we will be using the definition of a diva as a person who is larger-than-life, demanding, dominant, and overbearing; someone who takes away your space and makes you feel small. We will also be using the word "diva" to describe other personality types that you may find difficult — even if they don't conform to the stereotypical "diva" definition.

The over-bearing type of diva is just one of many difficult personality types. A highly dominant person may actually prefer to work with someone who is strong and dominant. They can relate to them better, because their personalities are similar. For this person, a perfectionist who never says anything and has difficulty making decisions may be the challenging personality with whom they have to work. Or the person at the desk next to yours who is constantly wanting to chat with you may be your challenging person!

In this book we are going to address all of these different personality types and give you tools to get along better with each of them.

> For the purposes of this book we will be using the definition of a diva as a person who is larger-than-life, demanding, dominant, and overbearing; someone who takes away your space and makes you feel small. We will also be using the word "diva" to describe other personality types that you may find difficult — even if they don't conform to the stereotypical "diva" definition.

Step-by-step we will go through the process of better understanding your situation, so that you can dramatically improve the working environment and conditions in your team or organization. It will help you greatly reduce conflict situations and become a much more effective and productive leader.

THE DIFFERENCE BETWEEN A DIVA AND A PSYCHOPATH

Before we continue, I would like to briefly address the one personality type that we will not speak about in this book: the psychopath. Recent studies have shown that somewhere between 10% and 15% of people in leadership positions are possible psychopaths. Psychopaths are cold, heartless individuals who manipulate others for their own personal gain.

I have often heard the accusation from people in a conflict situation that the diva in the situation is a psychopath or has some other manipulating psychological disorder. Thus far in my experience, this has never been the case. As Babiak and Hare explain in their book *Snakes in Suits: When Psychopaths Go To Work*, you would not be able to recognize a psychopath at the outset. A true psychopath fits in, becomes your best friend, and does not create overt conflicts in a team. Their manipulation is much more subtle and almost impossible to recognize in everyday situations.

Assume, therefore, that the divas in your life are normal people with different personality structures than you. They may be difficult to work with, but there is hope that you can build a strong working relationship with them. They may even desire it as much as you do!

WHY CAN'T I JUST BECOME A DIVA MYSELF?

If you would like to, you can become a diva yourself. In the operatic world we are taught from the beginning of our education as opera singers to fight: to *be* divas. As one of my voice teachers told me after I had an unpleasant encounter with a well-known, albeit unhappy diva, "You have to give others the impression of biting harder, faster, and deadlier than they do. Then you will be respected and left alone."

It reminded me of Fonzie in the old television show *Happy Days*. Fonzie was giving advice to Richie on how to be respected. He said, "In order to be respected, you have to have hit someone in your life."

This solution of becoming a diva yourself is popular in some circles. I've heard of several trainers who are literally teaching their clients to become divas. This is all well and good, but it is not a long-lasting solution to conflict situations. Depending on the personality structure of those being trained, they may instead come across as inauthentic and affected. They won't appear strong and challenging, just weak and comical. It may even cause them to lose the trust and respect of their peers.

Just think about what would have happened had Jeff and his team decided to take this approach: you would have a team full of unhappy divas! Because they did not like or respect the behavior of the diva, they would not have liked or respected themselves in this role. They would have felt incredibly uncomfortable, and it would have been absurd.

What's worse, the team would not have reached its goals.

THE ALTERNATIVE

A better solution to the situation is not becoming a diva yourself, but becoming more mindful of the situation of the divas around you and of the power of your own presence. True presence is a wonderful combination of inner presence — the ability to be in the here and now — and outer presence — the ability to own the room.

True presence is something that everyone can and should have. When you have the ability to stay centered and focused in difficult situations. You have a strength and confidence that makes you poised and persuasive. This strength and confidence is just one of the things we will work on in this book.

HOW DO WE BEGIN?

Before we embark on this journey of dealing with divas, it is important to know what you are getting into.

This book is designed to give you *real* solutions to *real* problems.

Jeff is absolutely lost. His team is on the verge of falling apart. He needs to bring them together and help them focus on reaching their goals. He is losing precious time and energy dealing with personality conflicts when he needs to be focusing on his team's project.

Step by step we help him bring the team together. The team members begin to understand their differences and how to turn these differences into an unstoppable work force. They learn how to turn what was once their greatest weakness into their greatest strength.

> Become aware of the power of your own presence. It is beautiful, and it is unstoppable -- even by your diva!

"Desire is the key to motivation, but it's determination and commitment to an unrelenting pursuit of your goal - a commitment to excellence - that will enable you to attain the success you seek."

— Mario Andretti, Champion racing driver

They begin to see how the qualities that once held them back are the same qualities that drive them to succeed.

The team members become much more actively engaged. They are more relaxed and creative. They experience less absenteeism and burn-out. They have more energy to concentrate on the tasks at hand and to get the job done.

As for Jeff, he, too, is much more relaxed. He begins to enjoy going to work again and being with his team. He no longer feels helpless to change the situation, because he has concrete tools that he can use to motivate his team and to help them better communicate with each other. He is able to spend his time and energy concentrating on his work and not on the conflicts in his team. He is finally able to lead his team to success.

If you just want a book that complains about how difficult some people can be, then this book is not for you. If you want a book that only blames the difficult people around you, then this book is not for you. If, however, you are looking for real solutions to difficult situations, solutions that you can implement immediately, continue reading. I look forward to working with you!

THE SOLUTION BEGINS WITH YOU!

The very first step to finding a way to deal with your diva is to commit to working your way through all of the steps in this book. They are laid out in such a way that you will have the maximum success possible.

We will begin with an analysis of the situation. Then we will look at goal-setting and how this will give the situation clarity and direction.

After that we will turn to *you*. You will learn how to be centered and focused. You will learn what may be triggering certain reactions from your past, and above all, you will learn how to remain calm, centered and focused — no matter what comes at you.

We will then turn our attention to the diva. Communication is like a bridge that we build to another person, and the foundations for the bridge on each side have to be strong for the bridge to hold. You and the other person are these foundations. If you or they feel weak or insecure, your "bridge" will not hold. Miscommunications are destined to happen.

Our job is first and foremost to help you be strong. Then we will find ways to help the diva be strong. We will do this by understanding and connecting to the diva as well as possible. When both of you are strong, a healthy communication bridge can be built. And who knows? You may even end up liking each other or become friends.

Oh, do you remember my story about *The Merry Wives of Windsor*, where the soprano blocked my bow? Well, now over twenty years later, we are close friends and very good colleagues. I would gladly sing with her anytime. I have never mentioned to her what happened that night, and I doubt that she even noticed what she did. Funny thing is that not too long ago, she was complaining to me about another soprano who upstaged her. "What a diva!" she said. I just had to smile.

QUESTIONS FOR REFLECTION:

In looking at the situation you have chosen to work on in this book, how would you describe your relationship to your "diva"? Is there more than one person with whom you are having difficulties?

_____

_____

_____

_____

_____

_____

If you could better understand how they tick, how would this help you in the situation?

_____

_____

_____

_____

_____

_____

If you manage to improve the relationship to the point where communication flows and the working environment drastically improves, how will this help you?

_____

_____

_____

_____

_____

_____

What are some other benefits of an improved working environment? How will you be viewed by your peers? By your boss?

_____

_____

_____

_____

_____

_____

Why is your success so important in this situation? In what ways could this success help you — both in your personal and professional lives?

_____

_____

_____

_____

_____

_____

_____

_____

Chapter 3

How Divas Play with Your Mind

In order to improve your relationship to your diva, it is important to understand how the diva plays with your mind. To accomplish this it is important to understand how your mind works.

At any given moment we are bombarded with billions of pieces of information that our minds have to filter through. Take a moment to look around you. What do you see? Try to take in as many details as possible. Do you see a table? Chairs? The room? A floor? Doors? Windows? Colors? People? Clothes? It can be overwhelming, and that's just the immediate information near you at the visual level. What about the auditory level? What do you hear? And what do you feel?

All of this information around you is constantly bombarding your brain and being processed by your subconscious.

Your subconscious mind takes in everything around you and filters out the relevant information to your conscious mind. This relevant information changes according to what is important or necessary for you at any given moment.

TRIGGERS OR ANCHORS

So what does understanding our filters have to do with our divas? Our filters control the information our conscious mind experiences, perceives, and processes. This, in turn, controls the emotional reaction we experience to people, places, and things.

Have you ever heard a song on the radio, and suddenly been taken back to a wonderfully romantic memory from your past? Or do you have a certain comfort food you like to eat when you are feeling down? The song or food are so-called triggers or anchors. An anchor is simply an external event or occurrence through sight, sound, or touch that triggers an emotional reaction.

Here's an example of how triggers or anchors work:

Last week I am trying to get some paperwork done at the city hall, and the city clerk is not willing to help me at all. She says I didn't fill out the right form, and instead of giving me the right form, she says

Anchors are external events or occurrences through sight, sound, or touch that trigger an emotional reaction.

that I should be able to find it "over there" on the rack of forms. After I tell her the form she mentioned was not on the rack, she retorts, "That's your problem!"

I am furious! After arguing unsuccessfully with her for almost what seemed like an hour, I leave resolving to contact her boss as soon as I get home.

Yesterday, I am walking down the street feeling absolutely great, and out of the blue I see someone who looks just like the clerk. Suddenly, I am reminded of the woman at the city hall. I begin to think about the argument we had and how much of my time she had wasted. I become angry all over again. My body becomes tense, I tighten my jaw and my step becomes heavy. I find myself physically re-living the situation from last week.

What is happening here? The woman I see isn't even the city clerk. She just reminds me of her. Why, then, am I so angry?

Let's take a closer look at what is happening — because understanding this process and how to control it will be invaluable to you in dealing with your diva!

HOW ANCHORS ARE SET

Our inner thought processes — what we think about someone or something — have a direct influence on our inner state, which in turn has a direct influence on our physiology. The more emotional our encounter, the stronger the reaction.

So with the woman who is triggering the memory of the clerk, I am reminded of the conflict situation, and I begin to mentally re-live that argument (thought processes). This in turn influences my inner state and causes me to become angry again. That anger causes me to tense up — it influences my physiology. This entire process occurs in a fraction of a second, and most of the time we are totally unaware of what is happening.

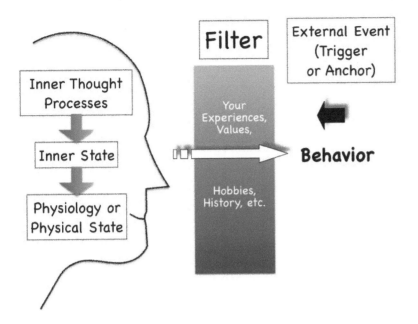

Over the course of time, we subconsciously set thousands of these types of anchors or triggers. Unbeknownst to our conscious mind, we combine objects, songs, people, and places with different emotional states that, in turn, control us. They control how we react emotionally (and physically) to different situations. We believe that we, our conscious self, are in control of our lives, but much of the time we are actually controlled from the outside, from factors that are subconsciously interpreted from the filters we subconsciously create.

ANCHORS AND OUR DIVAS

So what does this have to do with our divas?

Take a moment to close your eyes and imagine situations in which you encounter your diva. What emotions do you experience? Anger? Frustration? Impatience? At what point in your encounter with your diva do these emotions begin to swell up in you? Do these emotions first rise up when you see the diva or perhaps when you enter your building at work? What could be possible triggers for you in your relationship with the diva?

Take a moment and write down when you most strongly feel upset, anger, etc. (whatever your emotion is or emotions are when you deal with your diva).

_____

_____

_____

Now, pick one of these situations to look at a bit more closely, and put yourself in this situation.

While imagining the situation, go backwards in time to the point right before your emotions begin to rise. Once you reach this point, begin going forward in time in your mind. At what point do you begin to feel the emotion or emotions? What is it the experience — what do you see, hear, feel, taste or smell — that triggers the emotion or emotions?

Do this exercise several times until you find the triggers that cause your emotions to change. Please write the triggers (or anchors) here:

_____

_____

_____

Once you begin to recognize what triggers your feelings about your diva, you will gain control over the situation.

One last thing about triggers or anchors before we talk about the basics of communication. In the example above at the city hall, we saw how the trigger or anchor influenced my *thought processes* which in turn influenced inner state which then influenced my *physiology*. Fortunately for us, it can also go in the other direction: the *physiology* can influence the *inner state* which in turn influences the thought *processes*.

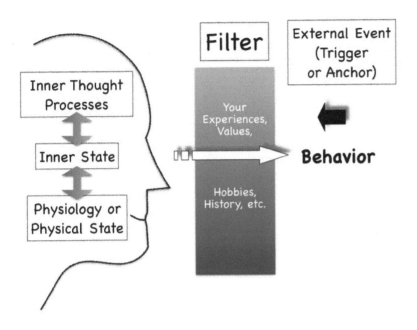

TRY THIS:

Stand up, look at the floor, and let your shoulders sag, really slump. Then say the words, "I'm doing great."

Now stretch your arms way up, look to the sky, and say, "I'm miserable."

Do you notice how strange it feels when the thought processes don't match the body language? Our thought processes do not know how to function when our physiology expresses something totally different! Mastering your physiology helps you to be strong, calm, centered, and focused. It helps you to get the job done.

In the course of our work together I will give you tools both to alter your thought processes and to master your physiology. In chapters nine through thirteen we will look more closely at how you can use these tools to remain calm, centered and focused. You can apply these tools every time you begin to feel controlled by your diva.

You have the power and ability to become consciously aware of the anchors that trigger your emotions, and, in turn decide whether or not you wish to be controlled by them. You control your emotional destiny!

"I'm an actor who believes we all have triggers to any stage of emotion. It's not always easy to find but it's still there."

— Hugh Jackman,
Actor, singer, producer

EXERCISE:

What are some possible anchors in your life? List those that you are aware of here — both positive and negative anchors:

_____

_____

_____

_____

_____

_____

_____

_____

_____

_____

_____

_____

_____

_____

_____

_____

_____

_____

_____

_____

_____

_____

_____

Chapter 4

Basics about Communicating with Divas

Communication
begins with you.

The word communication comes from the Latin word *communis*, which means to give information, to do things together, to share ideas and information, and to unify. If communication is a bridge that we build between two people or groups of people, it is essential that not only, as mentioned before, both foundations are strong, but also that both sides know what materials will be used to build the bridge. Both sides also have to know where the bridge should join together.

If you genuinely want to improve your working relationship with your diva, improving communication is the key. Communication begins with you. It would be nice — and easy — if everything were the fault of the difficult people in your life, and that *they* need to change. Unfortunately, it's not that easy...

When we talk about communication there's some good news and some bad news. Let's start with the bad news...

The bad news is that communication is always a two-way street, and we cannot try to change a system or relationship without considering our role in it.

The good news is that, in this process, you will learn more about yourself and how you can influence your world and those around you. This can be one of the most rewarding experiences you will ever have.

Bad communication happens everywhere — even in the most unexpected of situations.

A DAY AT THE OPERA

I was at the opera house in Nuremberg, Germany, for a rehearsal with a singing colleague for an upcoming concert. The pianist for the concert is a coach with whom I often work. We understand each other well and when possible, I ask him to accompany me for larger concerts or events.

Likewise, the soprano with whom I am singing is a dear friend and someone with whom I often sing.

After about three or four rehearsals, I realize that there is a lot of tension between my coach and my colleague. Little unnecessary comments start popping up, and we aren't making any progress. I begin to wonder whether we will be ready for the concert on time.

Around this time I meet privately to rehearse with my coach. Afterwards he says, "I love working with you. When I make a suggestion, you try it out. If you don't like it, you choose not to do it, but at least you listen to what I say. I have the feeling that our soprano just ignores me and does whatever she pleases. It's driving me crazy! At least she could say that she doesn't like my suggestions."

For those who are not familiar with the role of a vocal coach in the music world, the coach accompanies singers on the piano and gives suggestions as to how the singer should interpret the songs. Some coaches have a great understanding of how the voice works, others less so. This particular coach was in the "less so" category. He didn't understand that the suggestions he was making were beyond what the soprano could technically do.

He suggests some beautiful changes. The soprano does not implement them because she is physically not able to. He gets increasingly frustrated, because he believes that she is not listening to him. He begins repeating his suggestions and chastising her for not trying them out.

The soprano, on the other hand, is also getting increasingly frustrated, because she is genuinely trying to implement what he said. Unfortunately, with the technique she is using, she is not able to follow his instructions without her voice breaking away. As a result, she feels incompetent and belittled. And, even worse, because she feels incompetent, her technique begins to falter. Her voice begins giving her even more problems — problems where she has never had problems before.

While speaking with the coach, I explain to him that I know her and her voice well. I tell him that she is actually trying to implement his suggestions, but she can't do it vocally.

Once he understands this, he relaxes. He no longer takes her resistance as a personal affront, and he begins to find different ways to suggest an interpretation — ways that she is technically able to implement. She grows more confident and, although they never worked together again, the concert is a success.

THE FIVE BASIC RULES OF GOOD COMMUNICATION

Although this example comes out of the operatic world, it is very typical of the miscommunications I observe in many businesses and organizations. Two highly motivated people are trying to work together, but they simply don't understand each other. As a result they begin to dislike and distrust each other. Simple misunderstandings cause the working relationship to falter and deteriorate.

Using the story above, we are going to briefly look at the five basic rules of good communication. Understanding and implementing these rules will help you improve the working relationship with your diva. The rules may seem obvious, yet in my experience, they are anything but...

RULE 1: DO NOT ASSUME ANYTHING!

The first of the five rules of basic communication is do not assume anything. One of the most common mistakes people make is assuming that what they are communicating is crystal clear. Their ideas should be obvious to the most casual of observers. They also assume that they know what the other person is thinking.

The coach above could not recognize that the soprano was in fact trying to implement his suggestions, and he assumed she didn't want to implement them. Often we assume that the other person doesn't want to cooperate, even when they are sincerely trying to.

We see this type of assumption often when parents or teachers are interacting with what appears to be "rebellious" children. Instead of observing what other motivations may be affecting the child's behavior, we assume that the child is willfully going against our wishes. Of course, this may be the case, but more often than not we assume falsely.

For example, I am standing in the checkout line at a grocery store near my home in Germany. Directly in front of me in line is a mother struggling with her small son, who looks to be about three or four years old. After she finishes checking out, the mother starts pulling the boy's arm while saying loudly that they have to leave the store "NOW!"

The boy seems to not understand. Suddenly he starts screaming "No!" and tries to pull away from his mother. He manages to escape her grip, and runs toward the restrooms.

> You know what they say about what happens when you assume: It makes an "ass" out of "u" and "me."

The mother took pause, looked at her son in amazement and asks, "Do you have to go the restroom?"

He answers a resounding, "Yes!"

How often does that happen to us? We assume that we know what the other person is thinking and in this assumption forget to ask what their needs are.

The boy in this story — as the soprano above — wants deeply to cooperate, but he is not in a position to do so. His mother, however, chooses not to try to understand his needs and motivation. She assumes he is just being rebellious.

If, for some reason, you have to assume something about the other person, assume something positive. For example, assume that they have the desire to have a good working relationship. If the mother in the example above had assumed that her son wanted to go with her, but for some reason couldn't, she would have asked him much earlier what was holding him back. She would have saved herself, her son, and everyone around them a lot of stress. She would also have communicated to him that he and his needs were important to her — the basis for all good communication.

Even better is to never assume anything. Ever. You know what they say about what happens when you assume: It makes an "ass" out of "u" and "me."

PUT YOURSELF IN A NEUTRAL STATE OF MIND

In my seminars on body language interpretation, we begin with an exercise. I divide the group into pairs, and one partner is asked to leave the room while the other remains in the room.

I leave the room with the first group, close the door behind me, and explain the following story to them:

> *You had an awful week last week. On Thursday night you were to give a major presentation for your immediate boss, his boss, and several colleagues from your department. This was a make-or-break presentation. You knew you were being considered for a promotion, and this presentation could fix it for you.*
>
> *Unfortunately, everything went wrong. Your PowerPoint presentation, which had been working fine that afternoon, no longer functioned. The facts which you had stored to be electronically sent to each member present were somehow deleted, and you were not*

able convince those present that your ideas were of value to the company.

What's worse, you suspect that your partner (the person who remained in the seminar room) sabotaged your presentation. He is also up for a similar promotion, and he had access to the boardroom and to your computer just prior to the meeting. Now it is Monday morning.

I then go back into the seminar room where the second group is waiting, and I tell them the following story:

Your colleague (the person who is waiting outside the room) had an awful week last week. On Thursday your colleague gave a talk for the boss (you happened to also be there), and everything went wrong.

The PowerPoint didn't work, the projector had problems. Everything seemed to go wrong. It was especially awful, because he is up for a promotion, and this presentation would have been a deciding factor.

You really like your colleague, and you really want him to get this promotion. It is now Monday morning, and all you really want to do is to help your colleague feel better. We all have bad days…

I then bring the two groups back together again, and say, "It is now Monday morning, and you are just arriving at work. Please greet your partner."

As you can imagine, the people in the first group (who gave the presentation) are careful and distrustful when they greet their partners. Their partners, on the other hand, are cheerful. They try to cheer up their colleague.

What we believe about the other person affects how we interpret their body language and behavior. The members of the first group invariably misinterpret their partner's friendly, supportive behavior as suspect. They don't trust them and want to have nothing to do with them. And all their partners want is to cheer them up!

Even though we may not be willing to admit it, most of the time we go into situations, as the first group did, with presumptions and beliefs that influence how we react to the other person.

While a certain amount of skepticism may be helpful in some situations, if we really want to establish a healthy and effective

When dealing with your diva, there are at least three sets of goals happening at any one time: your goal, their goal, and the common goal, the goal that the group or team shares. The more precise you are about these goals, the more likely you are to accomplish them, and in doing so, you will create a win-win situation.

communication, it is necessary to free ourselves from as many prejudices, assumptions, and beliefs as possible.

It begins with you.

How you view the other person or persons is dependent on your inner state. Put yourself into a neutral state of mind, where you observe but don't judge or interpret the actions of others. This neutral inner state is only possible if you are congruent with yourself and with your own goals. We will discuss more about how to achieve this starting in chapter nine.

RULE 2: HAVE SHARED GOALS

The next rule for building good communication is to have shared goals. In music and theater this is easy. When we are asked to do a project, we know when and what we will be performing. The interpretation of the work still remains open, but the basic goal is there, and in most situations, all of the participants give their best to help to accomplish this goal.

When dealing with your diva, there are at least three sets of goals happening at any one time: *your* goal, *their* goal, and the *common* goal, the goal that the group or team shares. The more precise you are about these goals, the more likely you are to accomplish them, and in doing so, you will create a win-win situation. Setting these goals and helping you accomplish them, is one of the fundamental objectives of this book. We want you to succeed!

RULE 3: HAVE A COMMON LANGUAGE

Having a common language is one of the most important aspects of good communication. For example, every area of specialization has its own technical language that it uses in communication. This technical language is only one type of language, and if it is used in the wrong situation, miscommunications will happen. A lay person will not understand it. It is essential to know who is in your audience and how you can best communicate with them.

Using a common language goes even further than differentiating between technical jargon and a lay person's jargon. Finding and using a common language means being acutely aware of what the other person is saying and how they say it. It means truly listening to the other person. In chapter 22 we will go into further details about how to connect with others through a common language.

RULE 4: THE DESIRE TO COOPERATE

Also essential to successful communication is the desire to cooperate and communicate. No attempts at improving communication will succeed if one or more of the involved parties do not wish to cooperate. If someone truly wants to stand in the way of a project, they will succeed.

The reason that I have included this rule in this list is not because of how essential it is to the process. I included it because in my experience we very commonly assume that there is no desire for a solution on the other side. In reality, I've found this rarely to be true! Most of the time, even difficult people want to cooperate and to find a solution.

Think back to the beginning of this chapter. The coach assumes that the singer just doesn't want to cooperate. The mother assumes that the little boy just doesn't want to cooperate. All the people on Jeff's team believe that Stan does not want to cooperate — they believe that he wants to sabotage them! In all of these cases, those accused of not wanting to cooperate, actually truly and deeply want to. They just need help.

Unless you are unequivocally informed by the other party that he or she does not want to cooperate, assume that they do. Believe in your heart of hearts that this person has a stake in the outcome of your work together.

If you believe this, you will be much more willing to find solutions. If you discount the desire of the other person to cooperate, you will soon stop looking for the solutions you need in order to succeed.

RULE 5: TUNE IN TO WHAT THEY NEED TO SUCCEED

In addition, there has to be the technical ability to succeed. As in the case of the soprano, she wanted to succeed. There was no part of her that wanted to waste rehearsal time by repeating passages that weren't getting any better, but she was at the limit of her abilities.

How often do we ask someone to do something that they are not, in that moment, capable of doing? In doing so, we bring all of their abilities into question. This type of behavior on our part often leads to the other person feeling insecure and less competent. This, by the way, is one of the main causes of employee dissatisfaction and disengagement.

It is essential to understand the other person's needs. For us, effective communication didn't happen until my coach understood

> Too often we assume that the other person does not want to cooperate.
> In my experience, this is rarely true. Most people do want to cooperate and help the team move forward.

Be open to understanding other people's needs, and be truthful about what your needs are. For only when your or the other person's needs are met can you be open to finding solutions

the soprano. Once he understood the situation better, he was able to communicate his ideas in a way that made it possible for her to implement. Both could finally relax, enjoy, and make music together.

In the next chapter we will look at some of the most common situations in which people's needs are often not met. This will give you some insight into the needs that you yourself or your diva may have.

QUESTIONS FOR REFLECTION:

What are some situations in which you have made assumptions that turned out to be wrong?

_____

_____

_____

_____

_____

_____

What are some situations in which you have believed the other person does not wish to cooperate? Were you right about that belief? What happened?

_____

_____

_____

_____

_____

_____

_____

Chapter 5

What the Diva Needs (and You, Too!)

Just as we saw in the last chapter with our soprano, people often don't have the tools they need for success. I most commonly observe this in businesses that are not willing to invest in training programs for their new employees. They assume (again, do not assume!) that the employees already have the necessary skills or information they need to fulfill their roles. Some even expect employees to acquire the needed skills privately, on their own time and at their own expense. Not equipping employees with the necessary tools they need to succeed leads more to burnout than any other cause — and it leads to a discontentment which can cause misunderstandings and jeopardize essential working relationships.

EQUIP PEOPLE WITH THE TOOLS THEY NEED TO SUCCEED

But what are some of the basic tools that people need in order to succeed? The five most basic tools that every person needs to succeed in completing any task are 1) having the necessary **skills and training** to efficiently complete the task, 2) having the necessary **equipment** to complete the task, 3) having the information that they need to complete the task, 4) having enough time to complete the task, and 5) having a **corporate culture that encourages creativity and allows for people to make mistakes**.

At this point you may be thinking, "Why should I care about whether or not my diva has the tools they need to succeed?" Or the thought may even occur to you, "I don't really *want* my diva to succeed!" Just so you know, this is not just about your diva. It's also about *you* and *your* needs.

Our goal is to build a strong, stable bridge between you and your diva, so that you can effectively communicate with each other and accomplish the goals necessary for your team or your organization. As with any strong, stable bridge, the foundations on *both* sides have to be strong and stable for the bridge to hold. In this case, it is essential that *both you and your diva* have the necessary tools that you need to succeed. You both need to be strong.

"Success is no accident. It is hard work, perseverance, learning, studying, sacrifice and most of all, love of what you are doing or learning to do."

— *Pele, regarded as the greatest soccer players of all time*

As you analyze the situation with your diva make sure that you both . . .

1) . . . HAVE THE NECESSARY SKILLS AND TRAINING TO SUCCEED

When companies are willing to invest in training, skill development is the area they are most willing to invest in. Some examples of skill development areas include IT, sales, languages, change management, leadership, etc. These courses teach employees the specific skills that they need to function in the workplace.

Although we know that skills trainings are essential to build the confidence and efficiency of employees, statistics show that far fewer companies invest in skills trainings than they did thirty years ago. The need to have the appropriate skills to do the job is still acute, and this trend of cutting back funding leads to fewer qualified workers, more burnout and ultimately poorer customer relationships and greater dissatisfaction among both employees and customers.

Exercise:

Every business and organization — regardless of the type of organization (for-profit, non-profit, healthcare, church, etc.) — has different needs and different skills that their employees or members need to master.

For your organization, what are some of the skills your people may need?

_____

_____

_____

_____

What trainings would be helpful for them to make their jobs easier?

_____

_____

_____

_____

How would your organization benefit from better trained employees/members?

_____

_____

_____

_____

2) . . . HAVE THE NECESSARY EQUIPMENT TO SUCCEED

It seems self-explanatory that an organization should have the necessary equipment to help their employees or members succeed. A construction company without bulldozers or cranes would be unthinkable. This actually happens more often than you think. Not having the necessary equipment can mean anything from outdated software (or newly updated software that doesn't function correctly!) to machinery that is outdated or not functional. It can be as simple as not having enough copy machines or printers for your company's needs or having different divisions with incompatible software. Sometimes companies try to save money by not immediately acquiring the necessary equipment when in fact a lot of time, money, and energy is lost through this attempt at frugality.

We will not spend a lot of time here on this point, but before we go on, look at your situation with your diva. Could this point play a role in the tensions that are present?

Do you and those on your team have the necessary equipment (including software, etc.) to easily and efficiently do your job? If not, does this factor play a role in the tensions you are experiencing?

_____

_____

_____

_____

3) . . . HAVE THE INFORMATION YOU NEED TO SUCCEED

Stan, the CEO of a medium-sized international corporation, is interrupted by a phone call during one of our coaching sessions.

"The single biggest problem in communication is the illusion that it has taken place."

— *George Bernard Shaw,*
Author

Exasperated, he asks, "Why are you calling me about this? I've already explained it to you ten times!"

I offer to leave the room, but he motions for me to stay, indicating that the call is not that important and won't last long.

As he hangs up the phone, he says, "That was Betty, my new secretary. I thought she was going to be great. She was friendly, outgoing, and seemed competent when I interviewed her. But now I'm considering letting her go before her probation period is over."

"Why?" I asked.

"Look, I need someone who can think independently, who can quickly understand what's going on, and implement it. If she has to ask me about every single detail, I might as well do it myself."

He continues to explain that the previous secretary, who had been there since he created the company, retired two months earlier. She had trained Betty and showed her everything over a period of month, but for some reason this secretary has to ask him about everything.

I asked him what this particular call was about, and he said that it had to do with some travel arrangements for an upcoming conference.

"This is at least the third time I've explained to her what type of hotel room to reserve. I need to have a suite, so that I can hold meetings in the room. Why doesn't she understand this?" he explained.

In looking at the entire situation closer, we realized the secretary — who was intelligent and competent — was missing critical pieces of information needed to make these decisions alone.

The previous secretary had given her all of the factual information that she needed to be able to make these decisions independently, but she hadn't taught her the thought processes behind the information.

How she decided that Stan needed a suite in this travel situation and in another situation a single room was not disclosed. It seems benign, but it was adding stress for Stan. As a result, the new secretary begins feeling more and more incompetent with every passing day. She tries to err on the side of caution, and her boss cannot understand why, all of the sudden, he is being asked about things that in the past were decided by someone else.

I asked Stan in which areas of her work this was cropping up, and surprisingly there were only three or four types of situations where he expected her to be more independent than she was. All of those situations were ones for which a decision flow chart could be made.

We spent about two and half hours working on the flow charts for the three situations, and after that, Betty was in a position to take care of the situations on her own. She had the information she needed.

Information is not just facts that help the other person understand where you're coming from, but can also include thought processes that help the other person make better decisions. It can also take the form of references that help the other person find relevant information on their own.

In your situation, do you and the other members of your team have enough information to be able to work together well? How is the information flow? Are there areas where communications and decision-making could be more efficient and effective?

_____

_____

_____

_____

4) . . . ENOUGH TIME TO SUCCEED

One of the most important, though least discussed, tools for success is time.

You would think that in the digital age with all our modern conveniences, we would have more time than ever to relax and concentrate on the most important aspects of our workload. Unfortunately, this is not the case. In the information age everything is happening much faster than ever before and more information is available to make decisions. We put ourselves under pressure to always be available and to get things done faster than ever before.

In my experience, one of the factors that not only causes miscommunications but also recurring burnout is the lack of sufficient time to do a specific job. "It should be done yesterday!" is neither a professional nor responsible way to delegate responsibilities. But how often do we catch ourselves saying that?

Time is one of the most valuable commodities and resources that we have, and how you delegate and ration that time for a project helps clarify goals and greatly improves communication.

There will always be "emergencies" to be taken care of immediately and events that throw wrenches in our schedules. If, however, you plan most of the normal day-to-day procedures so that a realistic

> Time is one of the most valuable commodities and resources that we have, and how you delegate and ration that time for a project helps clarify goals and greatly improves communication.

time frame is established, you will notice that more work gets done, your team members are happier, and fewer "emergencies" will pop up.

And above all, make sure that you give your team the time they need to get the job done accurately and professionally.

Do you and your team have enough time to complete tasks with ease? Is this factor a source of tension in your organization?

_____

_____

_____

_____

_____

_____

5) . . . A PRODUCTIVE AND CREATIVE CORPORATE CULTURE

In discussing the necessary tools to get a job done, we cannot overlook the corporate culture. The role of the corporate culture in good communication manifests itself everywhere. The corporate culture affects the amount of time and funds allocated to training to equip employees with the technical skills they need. It also affects the flow of information, and how well time is managed.

Another important aspect of the corporate culture is how it impacts the handling of mistakes. It can be crucial in determining how courageous employees will be when trying new things out and taking on new responsibilities. If team members know that the corporation supports innovative thought and experimentation, they will be more likely to express new ideas. They'll also tend to insist on understanding the ideas that have been put forth, which in turn greatly improves communication and understanding.

In the June 2011 German edition of the Harvard Business Review (*Das Wissen der besten Harvard Business*), the cover article was on how companies can improve how they handle mistakes in order to encourage innovation. For example, the pharmaceutical company Eli Lilly actually has "Mistake Parties" to celebrate experiments that didn't work out. "Mistakes" led to popular products like 3-M's Post-It® notes and Scotchgard®, the Slinky, and Silly Putty. "Mistakes" also led to penicillin, ink-jet printers, and microwave ovens.

If the corporate culture does not allow for mistakes, however, employees become more cautious and less creative. They become afraid. This fear and everything behind it — blame, guilt, etc. — can cause unnecessary conflicts and tensions in relationships.

In your organization, how are mistakes handled? Are they a possible source for the conflicts between you and your diva?

_____

_____

_____

_____

_____

_____

_____

"Our number one priority is company culture. Our whole belief is that if you get the culture right, most of the other stuff like delivering great customer service or building a long-term enduring brand will just happen naturally on its own."

— Tony Hsieh, CEO, Zappo

If so, who is the person accused of making mistakes? You? Someone else (possibly the diva)? And what can be done to address both the mistakes and the tensions resulting from them?

_____

_____

_____

_____

_____

_____

_____

_____

D

I

V

A

**DEFINING THE SITUATION
WITH YOUR DIVA**

Chapter 6

Why Deal with the Diva?
Getting the Job Done!

The two main goals of this book are to help you remain clear, calm, and focused while dealing with your diva and to help you reach your goals in the situation with your diva. In order to get the job done — that is, to reach your goals — you need to know what those goals are.

When conflict situations arise, people often focus on the relationship and the difficulties created by it, and lose sight of the goals they originally wanted to accomplish. In Jeff's situation, his team began to concentrate on what they didn't like about Stan instead of finishing the project they were working on. Time and energy were wasted speculating on whether or not Stan would insult someone or block the progress of the team instead of focusing on getting the job done.

I should say, in all fairness, that it didn't start out that way. Initially, Jeff's team was focused on their work and goals. But as dissatisfaction with Stan began to creep in, the focus moved from the job at hand to Stan and his difficult personality.

WHY GOALS MATTER

So why do goals matter? And what does goal-setting have to do with dealing with divas?

When it comes to dealing with divas or other difficult personalities there are two reasons why goals matter. First, as we discussed earlier, if you and the other person have conflicting goals, finding common ground and reaching agreements will be nearly impossible. And second, you cannot focus on a goal if you don't know what it is. If you don't know what you want or where you want to go, how will you know when you have accomplished it?!

HAROLD

Harold, or "Harry" as his friends called him, is a project leader in a telecommunications company. Although he seems friendly enough,

"I don't focus on what I'm up against. I focus on my goals and I try to ignore the rest."

— *Venus Williams,*
Professinal tennis player

he can be very dominating and, if given cause, over-bearing. After telling him what I do, he tells me about his team.

"All I want to do is hold my team together so that we can finish this project, but it's not working. And there are at least two other companies doing the same research. We've got to win this one. Look, I don't care whether or not the team members like each other, but they have to at least be able to get the job done!"

Harry's goal seems clear. But is it really? And how did he communicate this goal? How can Harry get his team to actively pursue this goal?

Using Harry's example, we will look at how important it is to know your goals and the goals of those around you. You will see how we not only have overt goals that we can easily express ("get the job done!"), but we also have hidden desires or agendas that can often be very powerful in motivating us towards certain behavior or causing certain emotional reactions. Also you will see how important it is to establish a common goal with the other person(s) and to be able to clearly express and to focus on this goal.

SECONDARY AND HIDDEN AGENDAS OR DESIRES

With Harry his primary goal seemed clear: "get the job done!"

When I ask for details, he continues by saying that there are "a couple of stupid people on his team who just can't seem to get their act together." He feels like he has to do their work for them.

"Everything is taking longer than it should, and if we don't watch out, Team B (another team in his division working on a similar project) is going to make us look like idiots."

I ask him what the project involves and what has to get done, and I dutifully write those things down. I have the impression, however, that Harry's personal goals are different than just "getting the job done."

I ask him how he would personally benefit from the situation if and when his team gets the job done. Harry's answer is pretty revealing. He says he would get the promotion he has been working toward for some time now.

Outwardly, Harry's goal for the team is to get the job done. Inwardly, Harry sees this success as his way to receive more recognition and to get the promotion he has long desired. This recognition and the promotion are just two items on Harry's hidden agenda.

We always have at least one or more secondary goals which influence us when we make a decision, and often these goals or desires are stronger than those that we are able to outwardly articulate. Some common examples of hidden desires that we have are receiving recognition from others, being valued for our work, hope for some sort of change, etc.

The next time you are with your team, look around the room and imagine what their secondary goals might be. Ask questions about what they think about the project, what they hope happens in the course of the project, and what they would like to do after the project. From these questions you will learn how well the primary goal is understood by your colleagues and what some of their secondary goals may be. This in turn will help you motivate them and avoid miscommunications.

What are some possible secondary goals for you or for other members of your team?

_____

_____

_____

_____

"People with goals succeed because they know where they're going."

— Earl Nightingale,
Radio personality, speaker,
author

SHARING A COMMON GOAL

Often we think we know what the goal of the other person is. It seems obvious to us that their goal should be the same as ours. But it rarely is.

They have their own agenda, just as you have yours. It's your job to understand not only the common desired outcomes but also your own personal desires and those of your counterpart.

YOUR GOAL VS. THEIR GOAL

Even in healthy communication, people's goals may vary drastically. One thing is certain: if you don't know what your goal is, you won't know if you have achieved it.

So be very clear about what you want. The clearer you are, the better you will be at communicating it. You will also be more likely to succeed in achieving your goal.

Once my German husband, our small daughter and I were on vacation in London. We set off to find the next subway station to downtown. We had a map of the city, but it was not very detailed. We needed help.

"When it is obvious that the goals cannot be reached, don't adjust the goals, adjust the action steps."

— Confucius,
*Ancient Chinese teacher,
politician, philosopher*

My husband asked a passer by how to find the way to the next station. The friendly, charming person answered like this:

"Well, you could go this way (pointing left). First, turn left here, then take the second right. After that go two — no three blocks and … Or you could go this way (pointing right) and… What would you like to see? If you go this way (pointing left again) you'll go by the museum and park — oh, and the new shopping mall. This way (pointing right) is …"

By this point my husband was lost. In the attempt to give us all of the possibilities and the many sightseeing opportunities in the area, our temporary guide totally confused us. I asked which way was shorter, but the conversation just got more confusing.

Finally, we thanked our host profusely and walked on. We then asked the next passerby, "Would you please tell us the fastest, shortest way to get to the Underground. We are trying to get downtown by 5 o'clock."

This person answered our question in a friendly and, fortunately, succinct manner. We soon found ourselves standing in front of the next Underground station.

WHAT WERE THE DIFFERENCES IN THE TWO SITUATIONS?

Both people saw that we were lost tourists, but in the second case, we stated our goal much more precisely. We communicated exactly what we needed and what our time constraints were. In the first case we also stated our goal. We thought that it was absolutely clear. When we didn't get the desired answers, we refined our goal definition. Then, we got the information that we sought.

AND WHAT WERE THE GOALS OF OUR "GUIDES"?

The first person was well-meaning. He wanted to give us all of the possibilities, so that we could enjoy London and learn more about our surroundings. He saw himself and his own personal goals in the situation as being the perfect host — ready to share as much information as possible about where we were and where we wanted to go. These are noble goals, but they didn't help us very much, did they?

With the second person, we stated our goal more succinctly, and, as a result, the second person understood exactly what we were looking for. As a result, he made our goal his goal and gave us precisely the information that we needed.

It could have happened that the second person chose a different goal than ours. For example, he could have chosen not to be bothered by us and just brushed us off. He could have chosen to be as "helpful" as the first person and given us way too much information, or he could have told us that we didn't really want to go with the Underground, but would prefer a taxi . . . None of these would have helped us at all!

EXERCISE:

Think back to a situation where you felt misunderstood. What were your goals in that situation? And what were the goals of the other person?

_____

_____

_____

What situations are you experiencing right now where the other person's goals differ from yours?

_____

_____

_____

YOUR GOAL, THEIR GOAL, AND OUR GOAL

In our time together we are going to look at three desired outcomes which may or may not overlap: *Your* goal, *their* goal and *our* goal. Remember that with each of these, there are both overt, primary goals and secondary, hidden agendas.

WHY IT'S NECESSARY TO KNOW ALL THREE GOALS

Often I am asked why we need to look at all three goals. Is it not enough to know what the common goal, that is, what *our goal* is, and be done with it?

As you will see in the next chapter, Harry's personal goal is dependent on the success of the joint goal. Therefore, he is committed to the project until it is finished. If the personal goal of everyone involved is dependent on the success of the joint goal, then the task at hand is relatively easy. Everyone wants to reach the common goal for his or her own personal success. But what do you do if the personal goal of one or more persons is *not* dependent on the common goal? Or, even worse, if it is in contrast to the common goal?

"Setting goals is the first step in turning the invisible into the visible."

*— Tony Robbins,
Motivational speaker
and author*

For example, a common situation in which this occurs is when one of the team members is approaching retirement. Team members assume he will stay until their project is completed. But what if that is not the case? What if the personal goal of the team member is to simply ride it out until he or she can retire?

If the team ignores the goal of the soon-to-be retiree, they will certainly be surprised when he suddenly leaves. If, however, they have recognized the desire of the other person to go into retirement, they can prepare. Preparing might look like asking the employee to commit to the team until the end of a project or it might mean finding a replacement early enough so he can train the replacement.

Chapter 7

Your Desired Outcome with Your Diva

It is critical to understand what your desired outcome is in the situation with your diva. Later, after we have looked at different personality structures and motivational factors, we will look at the possible desired outcomes for your diva. Right now — and for the next several chapters — you are the focus of our attention. We want to be sure that *you know* what *you need* in this situation.

The miracle question from Steve De Shazer is a wonderful way of finding out what you really want in any given situation. When doing the following exercise, the one answer you may not give at this time is that your diva disappears in any negative way – no matter how attractive that solution may seem!

THE MIRACLE QUESTION

You are going to go to bed tonight, and during the night, while you are sleeping peacefully and deeply, a miracle is takes place. The situation with your diva is resolved. You encounter your diva, and you remain calm and centered. The goals that you had have been accomplished. The conflict is resolved.

Now it is the next morning — the morning after the miracle. You wake up, look around you, and are amazed at how beautiful and different things are now. What has changed? What is different from yesterday?

Describe the situation before this night (the situation as it is now):

_____

_____

_____

_____

_____

_____

"Review your goals twice every day in order to be focused on achieving them."

— *Les Brown, Motivational speaker and author*

Describe what has changed after the miracle:

_____

_____

_____

_____

DEFINE YOUR GOAL

Look at what you wrote in your description of the situation after your miracle. What is the outcome? What solutions are there to help you achieve this outcome? Who is involved in helping you achieve this outcome? You are well on your way to finding defining your desired outcomes and some possible solutions to help you get there!

When it comes to goal-setting, we know that people who clearly define their goals and keep these goals mentally present achieve their goals. But how do you define your goal so that you will achieve it quickly and with as few difficulties as possible? Here are two very useful goal-setting exercises that will help you clarify and achieve your goal faster and with greater ease.

Taking the situation with your diva and using the results you got from the miracle question, write down your goal(s) or desired outcome(s) in this situation:

_____

_____

_____

Is it just one goal or have you identified more than one goal? If you have identified more than one goal in this situation, please break the goals or desired outcomes down into separate individual goals:

_____

_____

_____

_____

THINK POSITIVE – YOUR BRAIN IS GOING TO ANYWAY

One thing to know whenever you are setting goals is that our brain does not register negations.

For example, if someone would tell you, "Whatever you do, DON'T think about a pink elephant," what is the first thing that you would think of? Most likely, it was a pink elephant, because in order to negate something, we have to first picture the positive form of it.

This is true of goals, too. If your goal is to not have any arguments at the family reunion, the first thing your mind pictures is arguing with someone at the family reunion — a sure fire way to program a few conflicts in advance!

One other point that strengthens your goal is to put the verb in present tense with the first person "I" or "we" as your subject. If your goal is to lose weight for example, then express it as "I am 15 pounds lighter."

If you write, "I would like to be fifteen pounds lighter" or "I will be fifteen pounds lighter," your brain continues to see the goal in your future. It is subconsciously unattainable. If you say, "I am fifteen pounds lighter," you are already in a state of being lighter.

By the way, one of the dangerous expressions of goals in weight loss is the word "loss." Subconsciously, we don't want to "lose" anything. The brain goes into conflict over protecting and pleasing the body.

Look at the goals you wrote above. Are they in first person? Are they in present tense? Are they positively formulated? If not, re-write the goal here so that it meets these criteria:

"Our goals can only be reached through a vehicle of a plan, in which we must fervently believe, and upon which we must vigorously act. There is no other route to success."

— Pablo Picasso, Painter, sculptor

SMART GOALS

Now that you have stated your goals in a positive manner, let's check them for other criteria. One of the best known methods of goal-setting is the SMART goal. SMART is a mnemonic device which stands for

S - Specific
M - Measurable
A - Attainable
R - Relevant
T - Timely

SPECIFIC

Look at the goal you have written out. Is it specific? One of the best ways I have found to make your goals as specific and tangible as possible is to ask yourself the six "W" questions:

Who: **Who is involved in achieving my goal(s)?**

_____

_____

_____

What: **What exactly do I want to accomplish?**

_____

_____

_____

Where: **Where does my goal(s) take place?**

_____

_____

_____

When: **When should my goal(s) be accomplished?**

_____

_____

_____

Which: Which requirements or constraints may be necessary to achieve my goal(s)?

_____

_____

_____

Why: Why is it important to me to achieve my goal(s)?

_____

_____

_____

MEASURABLE

Is your goal measurable? Will you know when you have accomplished it? If so, great! If not, what can you change to make the goal measurable? Add more specifics.

_____

_____

ATTAINABLE

Is your goal attainable? There are goals which are specific and measurable, but are not at this time attainable. Look at your goal and your resources and decide whether or not your goal is, in fact, attainable.

_____

_____

RELEVANT

Proof your goal for its relevance and sustainability. It may be important to you but not to anyone else. If this is the case, be prepared to let go of the goal — or see if there is a way to make your goal more relevant others who may be necessary for you to achieve the goal.

_____

_____

TIMELY

And finally, your goal should be grounded in a time-frame. State by when it should be accomplished. As in our example of asking directions in London, as soon as we gave a specific time frame in which the goal should be achieved, it greatly increased the probability of our reaching the desired outcome. By giving a time frame to your goal, you make it easier to assess your progress and you will find that everyone involved in achieving the goal will be more accountable.

_____

_____

HARRY'S PRIMARY GOALS

One of Harry's primary goals was that his team would "get the job done," but not because the job or his team were personally important to him. Harry was more interested in his own reputation. He was known as a go-getter, someone who could be brought in to motivate — or force — a team to get a job done. Harry was deeply proud of this reputation which was the reason he had been brought in to lead the project. First and foremost, Harry's goal was to protect his reputation by motivating his team to finish the project.

YOUR SECONDARY GOALS OR HIDDEN AGENDAS

It sounds subversive to say you have a hidden agenda, but you do. Really. And to recognize these hidden agendas will clarify your feelings and behavior in certain situations. It will also help you to understand the common goal you will establish with your counterpart. But how do we find our secondary goals?

HARRY'S SECONDARY GOALS

When I did the following exercise with Harry, it revealed much about Harry's behavior and motivations. Harry told me three possible secondary goals that were at play.

First, the project leader of Team B was a concern for Harry. Harry and this other project director had been in competition with each other for the past four years, and Harry wanted to show him up, proving he was the better leader.

Second, Harry was due for a promotion, and his immediate boss told him that if he manages to bring this project to an end, it would definitely "be good" for Harry.

Finally, Harry had worked with one of his team members before, and they had several run-ins with each other. The last time this team member had accused Harry of being a bully and had even reported him to management.

Now, several years later, Harry was having to work with this man again, and he was unhappy about it. He would prefer to fire this team member to pay him back for the past, but he couldn't. It was neither in his power nor would it be helpful. This team member had the necessary engineering know-how to complete the project. Harry wanted to be rid of him, and he didn't want this team member to receive praise for his work on the project.

How could he help his team "get the job done" when the main person who would be "getting the job done" was someone he did not want to be around and someone he did not want to succeed? Harry had a dilemma.

We'll come back to Harry and his team member in later chapters, but for now, take a moment to find your possible secondary goals.

FINDING YOUR SECONDARY GOAL:

Take the goal you set above with all of the SMART factors and write it here:

_____

_____

_____

_____

Now write down all of the positive things that may happen for you if you were to achieve this goal: (These may seem egotistical or even irrelevant. Don't take time to reflect on them right now. Just write them down.)

_____

_____

_____

_____

_____

_____

"I think goals should never be easy, they should force you to work, even if they are uncomfortable at the time."

— Michael Phelps, Olympic swimming champion

How could these goals — both primary and secondary — be influencing the attainment of your goal in dealing with your diva? Are your goals and desired outcomes congruent with the possible common goals? Or do they work against the accomplishment of the common goals?

_____

_____

_____

_____

_____

_____

_____

_____

_____

_____

_____

How can you improve your goals to be even more congruent?

_____

_____

_____

_____

_____

_____

_____

_____

_____

Chapter 8

Where, When, and How You Encounter the Diva

One of the first steps in dealing with divas and other difficult personalities is isolating the situations in which you interact with them.

Often when we have to deal with people we find difficult, we get the impression that they are everywhere, that they interfere with our lives much more often than they actually do. Our emotions cause us contort reality so that the divas seem to be everywhere. They end up coming into our homes when we tell friends and family what awful thing they did at work that day, they interrupt our coffee breaks by walking past us in the hallway.

To begin the process of dealing with divas, it helps to step back and observe how often we really have to interact with them, and to observe if our perception of them being almost everywhere is really true.

JEFF'S TEAM

When I began to do the following exercise with Jeff's team, I was amazed by the comments that came from one of Jeff's team members, Ann.

From previous interviews, I knew that Ann really only saw Stan at the weekly team meetings. And yet now, when we sat down to clarify exactly where and when Ann experienced Stan, he seemed to be everywhere! Ann was exasperated and didn't want anything more to do with Stan.

I asked Ann to make four lists: 1) the physical encounters she had with Stan, 2) the virtual encounters 3) a list of the other possible encounters, and 4) a list of the mental encounters that she had with Stan.

The Physical Encounters List is simply a tally of the times during the week (or month if necessary) Ann physically met or encountered Stan.

The Virtual Encounters List records the times Ann had virtual contact with Stan either through emails or other online media.

The Other Encounters List details other situations in which Ann encountered Stan, including such things as snail-mail letters, memos, or phone calls.

The Mental Encounters List tallies the number of times that Ann encountered Stan in her thoughts. This includes when Ann talked to colleagues about Stan, or any time she thought about something he did or said, or moments in which she had mental confrontations with Stan.

Ann's lists looked a little like this:

Ann's Physical Encounters List
- Weekly Staff Meetings on Fridays from 9:00 to 10:00 am.
- 1-2 monthly encounters in the coffee room

Ann's Virtual Encounters List
- 2-3 emails weekly
- The occasional Facebook post (roughly 4 - 6 times per month)

Ann's Other Encounters List
- Memos attached to a report – very rare

Although most of the correspondence between Stan and Ann was online or in person, she did on occasion receive a memo from Stan attached to a report. This was rare - Ann estimated once every two months or so — and it did not seem to cause much stress. It usually came in the form of an addendum to what had been discussed in the weekly meeting. Each contact was neither a surprise nor particularly offensive.

Ann's Mental Encounters List
- 3 - 4 times daily, usually in the coffee room when other colleagues would talk about the latest problems with Stan
- On the way home from work when reflecting on the day and how angry Stan had made several colleagues.
- Evenings when reflecting on whether or not the team will be able to reach its goals in the timeframe given
- When working on a spreadsheet and realizing that this particular aspect of the project was dependent on Stan's work
- Before the weekly team meeting when remembering with exasperation that Stan will also be there

The mental encounters list went on and on. For someone spending less than two hours per week in contact with Stan, Ann was wasting a lot of mental time and energy thinking about Stan.

When I asked her if those mental encounters helped her to do her work or to accomplish her or the team's goals, she said, "No, not really." On occasion there was perhaps a thought that was productive or useful, but on average the energy she was expending was not productive, and probably destructive.

By increasing her awareness of her encounters with Stan, Ann began to realize that the time and energy she had been wasting had little to do with her own work. It had more to do with wanting to support her colleagues.

I asked her if she needed to reduce the amount of physical or virtual encounters with Stan in order to be more productive herself, and she answered, "No."

SOLIDARITY

Ann's case is not uncommon. Often co-workers who may not even directly have prolonged contact with the difficult person may find themselves involved in the conflict. Out of a desire to support their colleagues, they find themselves being emotionally caught up in the situation.

The process of objectively looking at where, when, and how each person encounters the difficult person, enables us to open-mindedly evaluate the situation.

In Ann's case she found that once she realized how little she actually had contact with Stan — in comparison to how often she thought about the situation — she could take a step back from the situation and more consciously decide if and how she would get involved. She also realized that she had several things in common with Stan, which we will discuss later in the book.

YOUR SITUATION

Reflect on your situation with your diva. When exactly do you encounter them? Please answer the following four questions.

How often do you physically encounter your diva?

Please list all of the places you physically meet your diva (at meetings, chance encounters in the office, during coffee breaks, at the gym, etc.) and roughly how frequently this occurs.

Where do you physically encounter your diva?

_____

_____

_____

How frequently does this happen?

_____

_____

_____

How often do you virtually encounter your diva?

Please list all of the ways you virtually encounter your diva (emails, social media, Skype or other virtual conferences, etc.) and how frequently this occurs.

Where do you virtually encounter your diva?

_____

_____

_____

How frequently does this happen?

_____

_____

_____

How often do you have other types of encounters with your diva?

Please list all other types of encounters you may have with your diva (letters, memos, telephone calls, etc.) and how frequently this occurs.

Where do these other types of encounters occur?

_____

_____

_____

How often do you encounter your diva mentally?

_____

_____

_____

Please list all of the times that you think about your diva or carry on mental conversations with your diva. Also include times you carry on conversations with others about your diva, when he is not physically present.

What are the types of mental encounters that you have with your diva?

_____

_____

_____

How frequently does this happen?

_____

_____

_____

Look at your list of mental encounters and reflect on what purpose these encounters serve.

Are they to show solidarity? Do they happen to help you work through the situation? Reflect on how these encounters serve you. And reflect on how these encounters may be a distraction. Does this distraction serve you in some way?

_____

_____

_____

THE CONCEPT OF FIELDS

I first developed the Concept of Fields when I began stage directing. I found that my actors would step into their roles much later than I would, were I playing that role.

So I would ask them, "When do you step into your role?"

The response I would get was a stupid look and the answer, "When I step onto the stage."

My answer to that was, "Therein lies the problem!"

They were stepping into the role much too late. If you step into the role as you step onto the stage, the audience sees you — albeit briefly — as yourself, the actor, out of character. An actor has to get into the role much, much earlier. Depending on the role and the methods that the actor uses, he or she may be in the role days before the performance. At the very latest, he steps into the role while putting his make-up and costume on.

THE FIELD IS THE SITUATION

In my coaching work I developed the Concept of Fields further. In the theater when the actor stepped into his role, he entered the Field, or performance. In everyday life, it is a little more complicated than that. The Field is a variety of different situations that each of us experience in the different roles that we play.

Each of us has many roles that we play everyday. The roles of parent, partner, colleague, sibling, helper, and driver are just a few. Because we do not experience these roles in enclosed environments (as in the performance on the stage), we experience a variety of situations in every role we play.

For example, let's take your role as child. Each of us is a child of our parents. Even if our parents are no longer around or we have no contact with them, they are still our parents, and we are their child. For the sake of argument let's assume that your parents are alive and well, and that you have a relatively healthy relationship with them.

One possible Field would be when you call them up to see how they are doing. You are in the role of the child and the situation, or Field, is the telephone call. An entirely different Field is when you go to a family reunion. The role is the same — you are the child — but the situation is quite different.

FIELDS AND MINDFUL AWARENESS

Becoming aware of what Field you are in at any given time greatly increases your ability to be centered and focused. It helps you to note your mental and physical response at any given moment. You can then also recognize when you change roles.

The result is living fully in the moment and being prepared to react rationally to any situation.

HOW DO FIELDS HELP US WITH OUR DIVAS?

Let's look at how Fields help better define when, how, and where you encounter your diva.

Take one of the situations where you encounter your diva that you wrote about above and write it here (it can be a physical, virtual, mental or other encounter — important is that you only pick ONE situation):

_____

_____

_____

_____

_____

_____

What is your role in this situation?

_____

_____

_____

_____

_____

Now relax and allow yourself to visualize this situation with all of your senses. What do you see? Hear? Feel? Smell? Is there a taste? Write your impressions here:

_____

_____

_____

_____

_____

"Stay focused, go after your dreams and keep moving toward your goals."

— LL Cool J, Rapper, actor, and author

What you just experienced and wrote down is the field. Now go back in time to shortly before you entered this field. When exactly do you step into this role and this situation? When do you fully become this role in this situation?

_____

_____

_____

Which role and situation were you in right before you stepped into this field?

_____

_____

_____

When did you change over, leaving the first field and entering the second?

_____

_____

_____

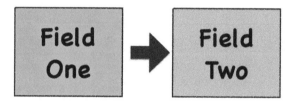

D
I
V
A

MASTERING YOUR OWN INNER DIVA

Chapter 9

Mastering Your Own Inner Diva

Now that you have defined your goals and when and where you encounter your diva, let's turn our energy to helping you find and master your inner strength.

Finding and mastering your inner strength means being able to remain calm, centered, and focused — yes, strong and confident — even in highly stressful situations. It means being aware of thought patterns and old habits that are holding you back.

In this chapter we will heighten your awareness of where are you are mentally and emotionally by looking at those things that take you out of your center and cause you to become angry, frustrated, or insecure. If we view communication as a bridge connecting two people, the bridge will only be stable if both sides have a strong foundation. Our job in this section is to help you have — and be — the strongest foundation possible.

We will then look at belief statements and thought processes that are holding you back from experiencing the success you deserve. We will look at how you can use your physiology to bring you into a positive state, and what the four most powerful states are to help you stay centered and focused when dealing with your diva.

WHAT TAKES US OUT OF OUR CENTER

It seems like it should be simple to be in the here and now. And yet, if I were to ask you to take a moment right now to be fully present — mentally, physically, and spiritually in this moment — you would probably find it difficult. For a minute or two you might find it easy. Then the mind begins to wander, to think about what you still have to get done. Where you have to go…

According to Richard Moss in his book *The Mandala of Being*, there are four things that take us away from being in the here and now: **the future, the past, "I," and "You."**

The emotions that take us out of our center and pull us toward the future are uncertainty or fear, or, on the positive side, infinite possibilities or hope.

Being in your center means being in the present moment, in the here and now. In the present moment there is no fear. You are safe. Fear itself belongs to the future and to the past. "What will happen if…?" and "When that happened the last time…!" are thoughts of the future and the past. Right now in this moment, you are safe.

Once you master being in the present moment, things become clearer and solutions will come to you with ease.

The emotions that take us out of our center and pull us toward the past are guilt, regret, or, on the positive side, nostalgia.

The emotions that take us out of our center and pull us toward "I" are self-importance or depression.

The emotions that take us out of our center and pull us toward "you" are anger, jealousy, envy, hurt, or on the positive side, being preoccupied with the other person, or codependent.

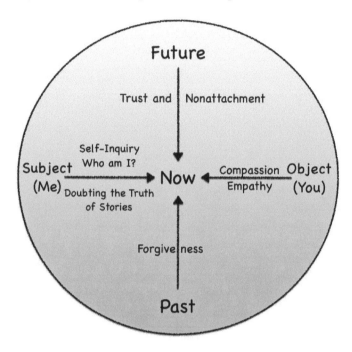

From *The Mandala of Being: Discovering the Power of Awareness* by Richard Moss, MD

The emotions or values that help us to come back to our center from the future are trust and non-attachment. To return from the past to the present it takes forgiveness, and to return from "I" to the present is self-inquiry. To return from the "you" to the present requires compassion and empathy.

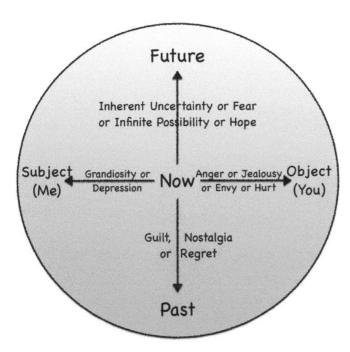

From *The Mandala of Being: Discovering the Power of Awareness* by Richard Moss, MD

In addition, the absolute basics needed to remain centered and in the present are a sense of joy, love, gratitude, and stillness and the ability to live in the moment.

THE FEAR OF MAKING MISTAKES

In my work on the stage and in corporations, I find that the two main reasons people get out of their center are their negative beliefs about themselves and their fear of failure, in particular the fear of making mistakes that lead to their failure.

Torsten Harder, a dear friend and colleague, is a classical cellist and composer who many years ago began exploring crossover music, in particular jazz improvisation. His work has led him to give improvisation seminars several times a year in which professional and amateur musicians alike come together to learn more about musical improvisation.

As I was telling Torsten about my work and the fear that people have of making mistakes, he told me about one way that he helps his students to overcome the fear of making mistakes. At the beginning of his seminars, Torsten has all of the participants come together and sit with their instruments in a circle.

He introduces himself, tells a little bit about the seminar, and then he asks each participant, one-by-one, to play the song they brought with them. He told me that at this point, you can see in their faces where they are — some are afraid that they are not good enough (focusing on Moss' "I"), others are worried about what the others are going to think. Still others know that they are very good, and you can see this confidence in their behavior.

Each person plays his or her song, and after each piece, the group applauds, and Torsten says, "Very nice. Thank you." He doesn't judge them or give any critical feedback.

After the entire group has played their songs, he says, "Thank you. Now we're going to do a few musical exercises to warm up, and while you are playing these exercises, I want you to forget everything you know about music. The normal rules of music don't apply here. Build in as many "mistakes" as you can. You should play these exercises as ugly and as awful as possible!" Usually at this point, the participants chuckle and make side comments about making mistakes and playing ugly.

Before they start doing these exercises, however, Torsten establishes several rules. First and foremost, he establishes an environment of trust, a safe space where the participants can try any- and everything without being criticized or ridiculed. He asks them to trust him when he gives them strange exercises to play, and he asks them to trust themselves so that they are free to explore and create without standing in their own way.

The other rules that Torsten establishes are that when the participants are playing the exercises as poorly as possible, that they allow themselves to be absorbed by the music they are creating, as if it were the most beautiful music they have ever heard or played. In addition, while they are playing they should solely focus on themselves and their instrument. They should be in the moment and in that moment nothing else exists.

At the beginning this is very strange for the participants, and they don't know what to make of the exercise. Why would I want to play in an ugly way or purposefully make mistakes? How can I concentrate solely on myself and my instrument with other people in the room?

Each participant goes off into their own corner and begins to experiment. They play the exercise they were given as ugly as possible. They begin to focus on themselves and their instruments, and while playing something so very unexpected, they and their music begin to transform.

After quite a while, Torsten brings them back together and asks each of them to play alone in front of the group again. In this moment, Torsten says the transformation is amazing. The hesitation that he saw from them at the beginning of the seminar doesn't exist any longer. Every participant is eager to play and to show what they have created. What they would have considered to be "mistakes" before the seminar are now exciting, new musical creations that only they are capable of unearthing.

In the course of this relatively simple exercise, Torsten totally changes the participants' perspective of making mistakes. Mistakes are transformed to music, ideas, and opportunities. The pariticpants relationship to their music, to their own creativity, and to their deepest feelings of expression are transformed and elevated to new heights.

MAKING MISTAKES IS OFTEN THE BEGINNING OF SOMETHING BEAUTIFUL

In the June 2011 of the German Harvard Business Review title article "*Aus Fehler Lernen: Was Unternehmen Besser und Schneller Macht*" ("*Learning from Mistakes: What Makes Companies Better and Faster*"), the author demonstrates that companies with a healthy attitude toward mistakes are more flexible, creative, and successful. Companies that have culture of reprimanding mistakes and suppressing decisions that can lead to mistakes tend to be less creative, slower to manage change, and less effective.

One of the companies that the article cites as having a healthy mistake culture is the pharmaceutical corporation Eli Lilly. The company actually celebrates mistakes with so-called failure parties. These parties were started in the early 1990s by W. Leigh Thompson, who used them "to commemorate excellent scientific work done efficiently, that nevertheless resulted in failure."

In 2004 the Wall Street Journal wrote this about Lilly's failure parties:

"Lilly has long had a culture that looks at failure as an inevitable part of discovery and encourages scientists to take risks. If a new drug doesn't work out for its intended use, Lilly scientists are taught to look for new uses for the drug."

They also wrote that Lilly developed "a formalized and thoughtful process in which it reviewed failures more honestly, more deeply, and started the process sooner than anyone else." This is a sensible response to what is reported to be the 90% failure rate for most experimental drugs.

As a result the researchers at Lilly are willing to take more risks and to make mistakes in order to find new products and improve old ones.

More recently in September 2016, the title article in the German *Harvard Business Review* again was about making mistakes with *"Aus Fehlern lernen — Warum sich Scheitern lohnt — eine Anleitung in drei Schritten."* ("Learning from mistakes: Why it is worth it to fail — Instructions in Three Steps") in which the author gives advice as to how to learn from mistakes so that the organization becomes stronger.

There are many famous examples of mistakes that ended up being success stories. Just some of these are Post-It® Notes, Scotchgard®, the Slinky®, Silly Putty®, Viagra®, Strattera®, and Evista®.

The adhesive for Post-It® Notes were discovered by Dr. Spencer Silver while he was trying to develop a super strong adhesive. Scotchgard®, also a 3M product, was initially created for airplane fuel lines. The Slinky® was discovered while engineer Richard James was trying to create metal springs to keep sensitive ship equipment steady at sea. Silly Putty® was discovered by James Wright in the attempt to produce a synthetic rubber for General Electric. Viagra® was originally developed at Pfizer Pharmaceuticals as a medicine for angina. Evista®, a $1 billion-a-year drug for osteoporosis, was a failed contraceptive.

PUT MISTAKES IN THEIR PROPER PLACE

In their book *Zum Glück fehlt noch die Krise ("Fortunately Only the Crisis is Missing")* Luitgardis Parasie and Jost Wetter-Parasie write that mistakes can be separated into four categories, depending on how high the consequences of the mistake are and whether or not the mistake is reparable.

The Mistake Matrix

out of the book *Zum Glück fehlt noch die Krise*
("Fortunately only the Crisis is Missing")
by Luitgardis Parasie and Jost Wetter–Parasie

	Highly Consequential	Lowly Consequential
Not Reparable	1st Degree Mistake	2nd Degree Mistake
Reparable	3rd Degree Mistake	4th Degree Mistake

"Sometimes when you innovate, you make mistakes. It is best to admit them quickly, and get on with improving your other innovations."

— *Steve Jobs, Entrepreneur and CEO Apple Corporation*

An example of a first degree mistake would be a pilot who is about to make an emergency landing. If the pilot were to make a mistake at this point, the consequences would be extremely high. Most likely everyone on board would die and the mistake would not be reparable.

My question for you: How often do you treat a fourth degree mistake as if it were a first degree mistake? In what situations are you most likely to do this? In what situations can you more easily let go?

A LESSON FROM THE THEATER

One of the most important things to learn when performing on stage is to cover your mistakes. The idea is not to try not make any of course. When they happen though, performers must cover the mistakes so that the audience does not notice. If an actor shows their mistake, the audience is pulled out of the storyline. The fantasy we have worked so hard to establish on stage is then destroyed, and the audience focuses in that moment on the actor, not the character.

The same is true when giving a presentation or conversing with others. Often we focus so strongly on ourselves and the possible mistakes we might make or have made that we don't allow ourselves to live in the moment. We put ourselves — both positively and negatively — above the other person.

I am not of the opinion that you should never show a mistake in interacting with others. Actually, there are times when it will strengthen your relationship and increase trust by admitting that something went wrong and that you would like to fix it. Taking personal responsibility for your actions — both successes and mistakes — is essential in building trusting relationships.

It is important at all times to be aware of what your goal is. When faced with a situation in which you have or may make a mistake, ask yourself how relevant the mistake is. If it blocks you from achieving your goals, then correct it. If by not mentioning it you damage the trust in the relationship, correct it.

If, however, the mistake is irrelevant (except to your ego) or if by discussing the mistake you will in some way confuse or distract your audience, then leave it. Cover up the mistake so that no one except for you will notice that it happened.

Too often I have experienced people giving a presentation who apologize for absolutely irrelevant things. "Oh, I apologize, I don't have a blue pen for the flip chart." "Oh, I'm so sorry, I spelled that word wrong. I can be so stupid!" "Oh dear, the powerpoint presentation is not as good as I would have liked." Just fix it — if possible or necessary — and move on.

The most important thing in communicating with others is to be aware of your goals and focus on those, not on the mistakes.

WHAT TAKES YOU OUT OF YOUR CENTER?

Close your eyes and imagine a typical encounter with your diva. Now go back in time to right before the encounter begins and let time begin to slowly move forward toward the actual encounter. When do your emotions begin to rise? What are you focusing on? Using Richard Moss's Mandala as a guide, answer the following questions:

Are you focusing on the future? Focusing on what may happen at some time in the future?

_____

_____

_____

Are You focusing on the past? Focusing on some event or encounter from the past?

_____

_____

_____

Are you focusing on some aspect of the _other person_? How they look, act, smell, or talk? Or possibly on what they are saying?

_____

_____

_____

Or are you focusing on yourself? Perhaps that you don't want to look like a fool or make a mistake? Do you feel small or uncomfortable?

_____

_____

_____

Notice your primary focus (the Future, the Past, the Other Person, or Yourself).

FUTURE:

If you are focusing on the future, bring trust and love into your thoughts. Know that at this moment you are safe, and that you have the skills to face any challenge that may come to you in the future.

_____

_____

_____

PAST:

If you are focusing on what has happened in the past, let it go and forgive. Forgiveness is a process — not an event — and the first step is to decide to forgive. To let go of the anger and hurt that has happened in the past does not mean becoming best friends with your diva. It means consciously deciding to release the past, so that you are free to get on with _your_ life.

"Learn to get in touch with the silence within yourself, and know that everything in life has purpose. There are no mistakes, no coincidences, all events are blessings given to us to learn from."

— *Elisabeth Kübler-Ross, Psychiatrist and Author*

_____

_____

_____

_____

THE OTHER PERSON:

If you find yourself focusing on the other person - either what they have done or how they are — let it go. With this element, it is essential that you try to understand the other person and to empathize with him or her. The aim is not to be like or even to accept them, but to understand how they think and what motivates them.

Remember that how they are is their problem, not yours — even if it affects your team or how your team appears to the outside world. How they are or what they do may affect what happens to them professionally, but — and this is important — this is not *your* problem. If they have hurt you in the past, then begin the process of forgiving them for it. We'll look more at forgiveness in Chapter 13.

_____

_____

_____

_____

YOURSELF:

Are you focusing on yourself? Observe your thoughts: do you feel incompetent or small? Are you afraid of making a mistake? Or, do you believe you are far too good to be in this situation dealing with this type of person? All of these thoughts are destructive to reaching your goals.

Take a step back from the situation and question how different it would be if the thoughts and feelings you are now experiencing were somehow wrong. Accept that you are not incompetent or small. Accept that everyone makes mistakes. And, accept that you too are responsible for the situation being as it is.

_____

_____

_____

MISTAKES:

In dealing with your diva, are you concerned about making a mistake or in some way being perceived as a failure? If so, how?

_____

_____

_____

_____

Are you worried that they are going to make a mistake and by doing so embarrass you or your organization?

_____

_____

_____

_____

"Experience is simply the name we give our mistakes."

— _Oscar Wilde, Author_

Chapter 10

Mastering Your Belief Statements

Fear of making mistakes is not the only thing that takes us out of our center. In the next few chapters we will be looking at other factors which take us out of our center and make us feel insecure. You will look at the beliefs that you may have about yourself or the world around you and how they subconsciously influence you. You will investigate the thought processes that influence how you react in certain situations. You will experience how to master your physiology so that you remain strong and focused, and you will learn how to tap into the four most powerful mental states, which guarantee that you stay connected to yourself, your values, and your purpose.

In this chapter, we begin to look at the mental games you play inside your head. These will give you insight into how you subconsciously influence or sabotage situations. One of the strongest influences on our thought processes are the conscious and subconscious belief statements that we have about ourselves, about others, about life, and about the world around us.

> If you believe that you can do something, then you can do it. If you believe that you cannot do something, then odds are, you will not allow yourself to even try. If you believe that someone else can do something, you will immediately trust them to succeed. If you believe that they cannot do something, you subconsciously stand in the way of their success.

BELIEF STATEMENTS

Belief statements are simply thoughts or inner statements about ourselves or the world around us that we believe to be true. Belief statements can be positive or negative, and they influence both how we view the world and how we react in different situations.

Major league baseball player Leon Brown once said, "It all begins and ends in your mind. What you give power to has power over you."

This is especially true of belief statements. If you believe that you can do something, then you can do it. If you believe that you cannot do something, then odds are, you will not allow yourself to even try. If you believe that someone else can do something, you will immediately trust them to succeed. If you believe that they cannot do something, you subconsciously stand in the way of their success.

Belief statements manifest themselves in many ways. Just to give you an idea of some examples of belief statements, one typical example of a hindering belief statement that I often run into is, "I have no

Belief statements are like tabletops which require legs to hold them up. The legs of the table are events in our lives that reinforce a particular belief statement.

problem giving a presentation for small audience, but when I have to speak in front of a large group of people I get nervous. I can't do it."

What is the difference between the two situations? Only the personal belief that one situation is easier than the other.

MARY'S VOICE

Not long ago, a friend of mine called me up not knowing what to do about her daughter Mary. Mary, who is in the seventh grade, is panicking because she has to sing a song in front of her class at school. It is a test that all of the students have to do, but in Mary's case, her fear is making her physically ill.

In asking her mother why she is so afraid, her mother tells me that in the fifth grade her music teacher told her that she can't sing, that her voice is ugly, and that she is not able carry a tune. Now she has to sing in front of everyone, and she is afraid that she will make a fool out of herself.

Her mother asks me if I am willing to listen to her sing the song. Perhaps I could give her a couple of tips on how she can improve?

Mary comes over a couple of days later to sing her song. When she arrives at my house, she is petrified. Before we even start she begins to make excuses as to why it won't sound very good. I tell her how cool it is that she will be singing this song, and we'll just see how things go.

Mary sings fine. At first she is insecure and hesitant, but with some encouragement and a couple of quick tips, she gets stronger and more confident. Finally, I say, "Mary, you sing this song beautifully. Just go in there and have fun!"

On the day of her test, Mary aces it. Yes, some of the tips that I gave her helped her to do better, but what really did the trick was simply having someone who has as much "musical clout" as her teacher contradict everything her teacher had told her. I am sure that other people in her life have told her that she sings well, but she disregarded their feedback, because they weren't musicians. I just happened to be someone she was willing to believe.

Belief statements are like tabletops which require legs to hold them up. The legs of the table are events in our lives that reinforce a particular belief statement.

In Mary's case she had a tabletop which stated that she couldn't sing. The main leg for that tabletop was the music teacher's comments. There may have been other legs, other situations in which someone criticized her ability to sing, but let's assume there was only the one. That made the table rather unstable and, in this case, easy to topple.

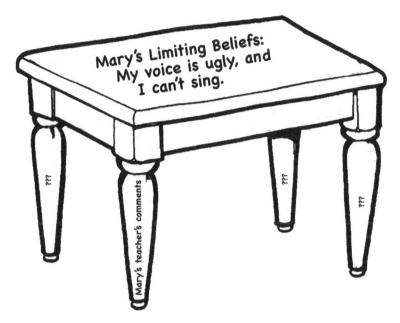

This allowed me to create another tabletop, also initially with one leg. On this tabletop was the belief statement for Mary "I have a nice voice, and I can sing well." I was lucky in this case that Mary gave more credibility to my comments than to her music teacher's.

I asked Mary if I was the only person who had ever complemented her voice, and she said, "No. My grandmother likes to hear me sing." As she thought further, she also remembered that a friend of hers had complemented her voice as well. Now she has three legs.

With three legs, the second table was more stable than the initial one, and she managed to quickly modify her self-image to match the second table. After she sang in school — which went very well — she had a fourth leg for her new table.

"Your beliefs become your thoughts,
Your thoughts become your words,
Your words become your actions,
Your actions become your habits,
Your habits become your values,
Your values become your destiny."

— Mahatma Gandhi, Non-Violent
Activist, Politician, Lawyer

In describing Mary's situation, it seems easy to change belief statements. The truth is that both tables continue to exist. There will be times, I'm sure, when Mary doesn't sing well, or when even though she sings well, someone will tell her otherwise. These experiences will continue to reinforce the negative belief statement. The challenge is how we enable ourselves to question the belief statements that limit us.

SETH AND HIS DIVA

Seth is a project manager in a large international corporation. When I first meet Seth, he is unhappy at his job because his division chairman, Bob, doesn't like him.

He says that every time he makes a suggestion as to how to improve the product line, Bob either ignores it or he tells Seth that idea is not feasible and cannot be implemented. According to Seth this has happened several times, and he isn't willing to stick his neck out again.

Since Bob brought me in to work with Seth, I knew Bob greatly respected him. I also knew that Bob liked Seth's ideas and found him to be an important contributor to the division. That Seth's view of the situation was so different from Bob's view surprised me.

I ask Seth why he thinks that Bob doesn't like him, and Seth immediately tells me several situations in which Bob ignored him.

Clearly, Seth has the belief that Bob doesn't like him, and he supports this belief with these examples.

I then ask Seth how would it be if he found out that he was wrong? At first, Seth fought the idea. He said that there was no way that he could be wrong — the evidence is clearly there.

I said, "I know. You're right. But just what if? Imagine for just one moment that you're absolutely wrong. Turn your beliefs about Bob upside down. How does that feel? What is then different?"

Seth thinks about it for a moment and then says, "It would feel good. If I thought that Bob actually likes me, that he actually wants to support my work, it would be a big relief."

I ask him again to imagine this with all of his senses and to describe what has changed.

As he imagines this, he says that he feels relieved, lighter. He feels as if he could go to Bob and share the status of his project without feeling like he would be rejected. He feels like he could make suggestions, and although they might not be implemented, they would be seriously considered. He feels like he would be in control of his project again.

I then ask Seth if there were times in his work for the division when he felt that Bob supported his work, and that Bob liked him. He said yes, and listed several of them.

"Believe in yourself!
Have faith in your abilities!
Without a humble but reasonable
confidence in your own powers
you cannot be successful or happy."

— Norman Vincent Peale,
Author and Minister

We draw two tabletops on a piece of paper and the legs that support them. To his surprise, Seth only finds about four or five legs that support his belief that "Bob doesn't like him," and all of these legs have to do with one specific proposal. For the second tabletop he finds at least six legs that support the idea that Bob likes him.

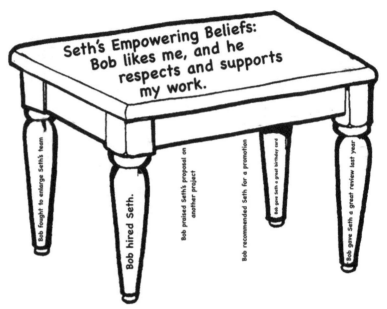

This revelation enables Seth to look more specifically at the problem, which is *not* related to his personal relationship with Bob, but is related to this specific proposal. It gives him the distance he needs to analyze the situation, and to be able to talk to Bob specifically about the issues that are causing Bob to react so negatively.

BELIEF STATEMENT EXERCISE — SO WHAT IS STANDING IN YOUR WAY?

Choose a difficult situation that you would like to work on. It can be a conflict where the communication isn't functioning or just a stressful situation that you would like to change. Take a moment to write down a short description of the situation and those involved. The best example to choose is a situation that is recurring.

_____

_____

_____

When you think about this situation, how do feel? Put yourself into the situation you would like to work on, and experience it with all of your senses. What do you see? What do you hear? How and what do you feel?

_____

_____

_____

In thinking about this situation, what do you believe to be absolute truths? These "truths" are easily recognized by the language you use when describing the situation or the people involved. When you hear yourself using words like "always" or "never," you are dealing with set belief statements. (i.e., "He is always like that." "She never does what she is asked." "It always rains when we…")

What are some of the belief statements that you have about this situation?

_____

_____

_____

Now create a table with their supporting legs to prove one of these belief statements.

"Commitment, belief and positive attitude are all important if you're going to be a success, whether you're in sports, in business or, as in my case, anthropology."

— *Donald Johanson, Paleoanthropologist*

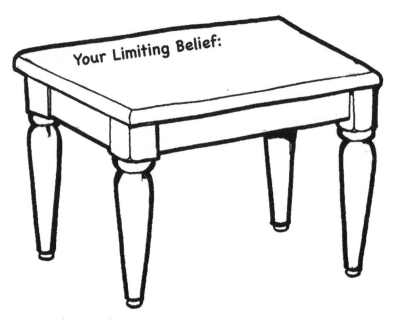

Now that you have done this, turn each table on its head, so to speak. Create tables with a belief statement that is the opposite of your original tables and find arguments that support these new belief statements — these statements are the opposite of your original suppositions. For example, if your original statement was, "He doesn't like me." Your statement would now be, "He likes me." If it was, "He's a jerk." It would now be, for example, "He's a great guy with many positive attributes."

_____

_____

_____

_____

_____

_____

_____

_____

_____

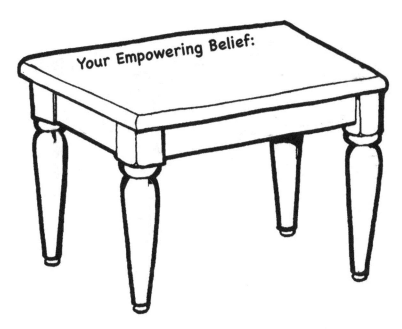

Just for a moment, act as if these new statements are genuinely true, as if you have been wrong, completely wrong, the entire time. How would you feel if these new statements were the truth? What would change? How would this change the situation? How would this change your relationship to the people around you?

_____

_____

_____

_____

_____

BELIEF STATEMENTS AND OUR DIVAS

Now, what do belief statements have to do with the situation with our divas? As in the situation with Bob and Seth, we often believe things about ourselves or about other people that may not be true. Just as Seth realized that there was substantial evidence to support the fact that Bob likes him, we are going to look at your situation to see if we can challenge your belief statements. To see if we can help you be more effective in relating to your diva.

Our beliefs about ourselves are so important because ultimately they are what shape and create our dreams and our lives.

Let's do the exercise that we did above, but this time — if you haven't already done so — we will use a situation involving your diva. The most effective way to do this is by writing down something that you believe to be true about your diva directly. (For example, statements like, "He is dumb." "She is lazy." "He is not an effective worker.")

Write down the situation in which you most commonly (or emotionally) encounter your diva. What are some possible belief statements that you have about him or her?

_____

_____

_____

_____

When you think about this situation, how do feel? Put yourself into the situation you would like to work on, and experience it with all of your senses. What do you see? What do you hear? How and what do you feel?

_____

_____

_____

_____

In thinking about this belief statement, what do you believe to be absolute truths? These "truths" are easily recognized by the language you use when describing the situation or the people involved. When you hear yourself using words like "always" or "never," you are dealing with set belief statements. (i.e., "He is always like that." "She never does what she is asked." "It always rains when we… ")

What are some of the belief statements that you have about him or her?

_____

_____

_____

_____

Now create tables with their supporting legs to prove each of these belief statements.

Now that you have done this, turn each table on its head, so to speak. Create tables with a belief statement that is the opposite of your original tables and find arguments that support these new belief statements.

Your mind manifests everything before it happens. Your thoughts become reality. What you believe about yourself is what you will ultimately allow yourself to become.

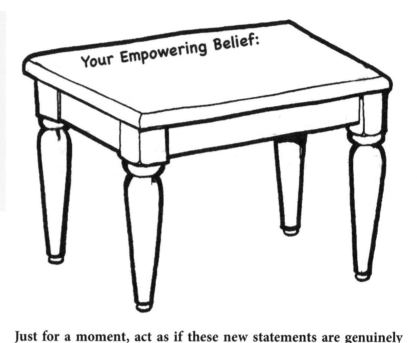

Your Empowering Belief:

Just for a moment, act as if these new statements are genuinely true, as if you have been wrong, completely wrong, the entire time. How would you feel if these new statements were the truth? What would change? How would this change the situation? Your relationship to the people around you? To your diva?

_____

_____

_____

_____

_____

_____

_____

_____

Chapter 11

Mastering Your Thought Processes

Once you begin to recognize those things which take you out of your center and you understand what your conscious and subconscious belief statements are, you are well on your way to mastering your inner thought processes. Once you master your inner thought processes, you are well on your way to being able to deal with your diva in a relaxed and professional manner.

In this chapter we will look at two basic things that will help you focus in on your thought processes. 1) Connecting to your sense of purpose and identity and 2) cultivating a positive mental attitude.

CONNECTING TO YOUR SENSE OF PURPOSE AND IDENTITY

Connecting to your sense of purpose and identity is helpful in remaining calm, centered, and focused. Think of well-known people who we as a society recognize as having a strong inner presence — those who, although they have gone through many trials and tribulations, come out on top with a strength that seems unstoppable. One of the things these people have in common is a strong sense of purpose and identity. They know who they are, and they know why they are here on Earth. They know what purpose they have to fulfill.

Once we know who we are — what identity, values, and purpose we have — how we react in difficult situations becomes much clearer. We stop reacting to things going on around us and begin acting according to our values, identity, and character. We become more pro-active and less reactive. Being proactive — taking personal responsibility for your actions and actively working toward your success — gives you a power and strength beyond imagination.

STEP 1: WHO ARE YOU?

From as early as I can remember through at least my college years, my father would say, "Laura, remember who you are" every time I left the house. This was probably the most powerful sentence anyone could say. What my father was telling me was that in everything I did and in every decision I had to face, I should remember

"Learn to get in touch with the silence within yourself, and know that everything in life has purpose. There are no mistakes, no coincidences, all events are blessings given to us to learn from."

— *Elisabeth Kübler-Ross, Author, Psychiatrist, and Pioneer in Near-Death Studies*

who I was — what my values are, what my sense of purpose is, and who my role models are — and hold this up as my standard.

As a result of his sometimes annoying comment, I had to consider the question, "Who am I?" I remember many times rolling my eyes and saying, "Yes, Dad." But even before my car pulled away, I began to ponder who I was and who I wanted to be.

In my own mind I set the standard for my life. I considered myself to be a good, responsible driver, so I acted accordingly. I considered myself to be compassionate and respectful, so I acted accordingly. When others offered me something like drugs or alcohol (as an underage minor), it didn't fit with the person I was striving to be. This gave me the strength to say no.

None of us is perfect. We all have setbacks that may not fit our own definition of who we are or who we want to be, but the more aware we are of our sense of purpose and identity, the stronger we will be in situations that challenge our beliefs or sense of identity. A person who believes that he or she can easily accomplish something will be much more likely to easily accomplish the task than those who do not believe that of themselves.

So, my question for you is, who are you?

Knowing the answer to this question will give you clarity and sense of purpose. Your values, talents, environment, behavior and history are all embodied in this person known as "you." And, as I mentioned above, what is also present in this question is an assumption that you yourself get to define who you are.

In that moment when someone asks you, "Who are you?" you get to choose exactly who you are — both who you are and, perhaps even more importantly, who you would like to be. The following exercises will lead you to finding your greater self and your sense of purpose.

EXERCISE 1: YOUR BIOGRAPHY

The first step in defining your identity and purpose is to write down your biographical information. With as many answers as possible finish the following sentences:

I am . . . (If you can't think of anything to start, just write your name or gender.)

_____

_____

_____

_____

_____

My parents are . . .

_____

_____

_____

_____

_____

My family is . . .

_____

_____

_____

_____

_____

Three people I hang out with most often are . . .

_____

_____

_____

My three most favorite hobbies and interests are . . .

_____

_____

_____

Five things I do really well are . . .

_____

_____

_____

_____

_____

Five different roles I play in my life are (i.e. parent, child, sibling, colleague…)

_____

_____

_____

_____

_____

Three groups or organizations I belong to are . . .

_____

_____

_____

What are five key events in my life?

_____

_____

_____

_____

_____

I am willing to fight for . . .

_____

_____

_____

_____

Where I envision myself in five years? Ten years?

_____

_____

_____

_____

_____

In the next exercises we will define your sense of purpose. Our sense of purpose in life comes from different factors that come together: our biography (as seen above), our abilities, family, personal and family history, our own personal story, factors that motivate us, and our core values.

As we go about our daily lives, these factors guide us, and we find ourselves in situations that shape our sense of purpose, our "why," so to speak. So as you do these exercises, ask yourself what *your* "why" is. Why are you here? And what are you supposed to accomplish here?

EXERCISE 2: CONNECTING TO YOUR PERSONAL STORY

Both your identity and your personal story give strong indications of not only where you have been and what you have done in your life, but also to where you would like to go.

FINDING UNIQUENESS

Read through what you wrote in your biography. Take three different color pens and mark in one color the things in your personal identity and history that have had the most influence on your past.

With another color mark the things you feel have the most to do with your future. What part of your identity or history would you like to be a definite part of your future?

With the third color mark things in your identity and history that make you unique.

Where are there overlapping elements, things marked by more than one color? Marked by all three colors? What importance might this overlap have?

_____

_____

_____

"Everything we do is for the purpose of altering consciousness. We form friendships so that we can feel certain emotions, like love, and avoid others, like loneliness. We eat specific foods to enjoy their fleeting presence on our tongues. We read for the pleasure of thinking another person's thoughts."

— Sam Harris, Author, Philosopher, and Neuroscientist

HIDDEN SECRETS

What we think is what we become. Positive and negative.

We often have ideas, dreams, and hopes that we keep to ourselves, either because we are afraid to mention them to others or because we want to keep them for ourselves, keep them sacred.

These hidden dreams can often reveal elements of our life's purpose. Is there any idea, plan, or desire you have kept secret? Possibly even something that you didn't want to admit to yourself? Could this secret be in some way part of your future?

For example, I always somehow knew I was supposed to go to Germany. I didn't know why or when or even how but I somehow knew that Germany was in my future. Because it seemed like such a far off, strange thing, I never mentioned it to anyone. The closer I came to going to Germany however, the more I understood about the why and when. At this point, it became less of a secret and more of a goal. (Even though I did not know how long I would end up staying and what impact the country and culture would have on my life!)

Reflect on how you think the important aspects of your identity and history could be part of your purpose. Could your hidden dreams be a part of that future?

_____

_____

_____

_____

_____

MOTIVATION

There are things in life that we simply enjoy doing. Revel in those things you love, and let these tasks or situations guide you to finding your purpose. There are things that consciously and subconsciously motivate or demotivate you. Both are indicators of your life's purpose.

Have you ever noticed how some things are just so easy to do? And with some things you can't wait to get started and to move forward. In these situations, where you feel a natural motivation, you're being gently led toward your purpose.

Things that motivate you can be as simple as being a morning person, eager to start the day. Or they can be more complicated like enjoying organizing or getting a thrill out of straightening out a chaotic situation. Recognizing which situations motivate you or make you most happy gives you insight to your value systems, your talents, and your purpose in life.

For example, if you love helping other people organize their chaos, what is it about this that you like? Helping the other person? The system that you develop with the other person? The feeling of satisfaction when everything is cleaned up and in its place? When you find that element of helping the other person organize their chaos that motivates you and makes you happy, decide how you can incorporate this element into your everyday life and work.

In the same way, the things that do not motivate you or do not make you happy also give you information about your value systems, talents and purpose. You may hate doing your taxes, for example. You still have to do them, but this shows that perhaps the job of an accountant may not be for you!

Recently I was asked, "But what if the thing that I like — that motivates me and makes me happy — is playing computer games?" Then ask yourself what it is about the computer games that you like. Is it the strategies that you have to develop? Is the manual dexterity? Is it getting to know other people online? Is it the competitive nature of the games? Is it the fact that you can play them at home, alone, in your pajamas? What is it about the computer games that motivates you and makes you happy? This or these elements give you insight to your values and your talents. How can they factor into your life's purpose?

EXERCISE 3: WHAT MOTIVATES YOU

Make two lists. In the first, write out five situations in which you are highly motivated. In the second, write five situations in which you are not motivated at all. What do these situations tell you about yourself and your values?

Five situations in which you are highly motivated:

_____

_____

_____

_____

_____

"I believe we're all put on this planet for a purpose, and we all have a different purpose... When you connect with that love and that compassion, that's when everything unfolds."

— Ellen DeGeneres, Actress, Comedian, and Talk-Show host

"Ability is what you're capable of doing. Motivation determines what you do. Attitude determines how well you do it."

— Lou Holtz, American Football Player, Coach, and Analyst

Five situations in which you are not motivated at all:

_____

_____

_____

_____

_____

How can you use this information to guide your everyday life and to help you find your purpose?

_____

_____

_____

_____

Now write down five situations in which you were most happy, followed by five situations in which you were least happy. What do these situations tell you about yourself and your values?

Five situations in which you were most happy:

_____

_____

_____

_____

Five situations in which you were least happy:

_____

_____

_____

_____

How can you use this information to guide your everyday life and to help you find your purpose?

_____

_____

_____

_____

_____

"Many persons have a wrong idea of what constitutes true happiness. It is not attained through self-gratification but through fidelity to a worthy purpose."

— Helen Keller, Author and Political Activist

YOUR CORE VALUES

Roy E. Disney, the nephew of Walt Disney, once said, "When your values are clear to you, making decisions becomes easier." This is true indeed. One of the main motivating factors in our lives is our value system.

In addition, understanding our values and beliefs helps us better understand our life's purpose. For example, for Mahatma Gandhi or for Dr. Martin Luther King, Jr., the value of nonviolence was highly important. By holding true to this value, both men led two of the most powerful and admired political movements of the twentieth century.

These two exercises will help you learn more about your values and about your life's purpose.

YOUR EULOGY

When your life draws to a close, what do you want people to say about you and the life you have lead?

_____

_____

_____

_____

_____

YOUR VALUES

Look at the following list of values (it is only a partial list, feel free to add to it!) and circle the values most important to you.

"When your values are clear to you, making decisions becomes easier."

— Roy E. Disney, Businessman and Co-Founder of Walt Disney Productions

Of those circled, pick seven values that are the most important to you. If there is a value that is important to you but not on the list, please add it!

Then strike out at least seven values that are not important to you.

What do the values that you have chosen (and those least "valuable" to you) tell you about yourself and the direction of your purpose?

Adventure	Humility	Reliability	Patience
Courage	Cleanliness	Helpfulness	Responsibility
Intelligence	Orderliness	Peace	Beauty
Family	Commitment	Purity	Friendliness
Creativity	Trustworthi-	Self-discipline	Moderation
Trust	ness	Gratitude	Privacy
Humour	Generosity	Honesty	Change
Understanding	Tolerance	Tact	Cooperation
Love	Contentment	Faith	Unity
Wisdom	Collabouration	Perseverance	Fidelity
Mercy	Tranquility	Joyfulness	Devotion
Forgiveness	Power	Acceptance	Self-acceptance
Gentleness	Innovation	Wealth	Accountability
Goodness	Harmony	Problem solv-	Spirituality
Competition	Responsiveness	ing	Empathy
Strength	Fun	Freedom	Quality
Knowledge	Progress	Good will	Challenging
Punctuality	Kindness	Practicality	Piety
Fitness	Steadfastness	Detachment	
Friendship	Balance	Discernment	
Righteousness	Preservation	Determination	

_____

_____

_____

_____

_____

POSITIVE MENTAL ATTITUDE

Many years ago, I was given Emmet Fox's book *The 7 Day Mental Diet*, and it was one of the shortest and most challenging books I've ever read. The challenge was to think only positive thoughts for seven days!

I know many people make light of the power of positive thought, but the truth is that our brain can only do either one or the other at any given time. And being in a positive state of mind is far more productive and creative than being in a negative state of mind.

Picture it this way: our brain has two filing cabinets. One contains positive thoughts and the other negative thoughts. When your brain opens the drawer to one of the filing cabinets the other filing cabinet automatically locks until the first filing cabinet drawer has been shut completely. So when you think negative thoughts, you do not have access at that moment to the contents of the filing cabinet of positive thoughts.

POSITIVE AFFIRMATIONS AND MANTRAS

One way to train your mind to be positive is to use mantras, or positive affirmations. Mantras and positive affirmations are simply phrases we repeat in our mind or out loud over and over again until they become integrated into our thought processes. They become a part of who we are.

At a subconscious level, we naturally repeat belief statements about ourselves (often negative ones!) constantly. By consciously training your brain to choose positive affirmations, you slowly change your thought patterns. You literally make yourself stronger. And as you observe what thoughts take you out of your center, you will become more and more aware of the negative belief statements that have been influencing your life all of these years, and begin to let them go.

Below you will find some examples of positive affirmations. Choose one of these to begin with (later you can add more) and incorporate it into your everyday life. Begin by repeating it out loud over and over again, and then repeat them silently in your mind.

Choose ONE:
- Every day in every way I am getting stronger and better.
- I choose love. Love is present in my life and guides my every deed.
- For everything I have and all I have experienced in my life, I am grateful.
- Nothing comes into my life as pure chance. I want to learn and grow from each experience.
- I am in the here and now. I am present. I am safe.

- For everything I have and everything I am, I am truly grateful.
- There is beautiful purpose for me in my life, and I openly walk toward this purpose in all I do.

POSITIVE MINDSETS IMPROVES COMMUNICATION

Miscommunications most often occur when we are in a negative inner state, and are not feeling good about ourselves. When we feel insecure we often project these feelings of negativity onto the situation or onto the other person. In order to reach an inner state where you can remain calm, centered, and focused, the first step is to recognize and control your ability to think positively.

So let's put everything together we have worked on thus far and apply these exercises to your situation with your diva. Take time to do the following exercise as often as possible, for only through understanding what inner peace and calm is — only through regularly experiencing it — can you know what it is that you are striving towards and can you find this peace of mind when you are in difficult situations.

EXERCISE:

Take a moment and put yourself in a comfortable seated position. Relax your body and close your eyes. Feel the floor beneath your feet and the chair or sofa on which you're sitting. Relax your head, your eyes, your facial muscles, and jaw. Relax your shoulders, your arms, your hands, and torso. Relax your hips, your thighs, your calves, and feet.

In this relaxed state, picture who you are and who you want to be. Your history, your values, your beliefs all make up that beautiful person who is YOU. Allow yourself a moment to reflect on your past and be thankful. Be thankful for the opportunities — both positive and difficult — you have been given and for all you have learned from them. Be thankful for the life and experiences that you have had thus far in your life, because they help make you who you are.

Now take a moment to reflect on who you want to be. Enjoy this moment of realization of all of the potential opportunities ahead of you. Enjoy this moment and be thankful. Be thankful even without knowing what they are going to be. Trust that the future will be much bigger and more beautiful than you could ever imagine.

As you relax further and reflect on your past and future, say the mantra you have chosen gently to yourself over and over again.

As you say it, observe what is happening in your body. How do feel? What do you feel? A feeling of calm should come over you, a feeling of trust and of letting go.

For some of you, this feeling may be short-lived, because you have doubts about your life or future. For others, you can hold onto these feelings of calm, trust, and, yes, love a little longer. Relish these feelings and stay in this peaceful state as long as your mind allows you — for at least five minutes if you can.

For some of you, you may actually feel overwhelmed. If this happens to you, return to concentrating on your breath and feel the chair you are sitting in and the floor underneath your feet. Say to yourself, "I am in the here and now. I breathe in and I breathe out." Concentrate on your breath flowing into your lower abs until your mind relaxes.

In this relaxed, centered state of mind, you can tap into your creativity, connect with yourself and also with others. In this state, you will find that solutions come easier and challenges seem smaller.

Practice going into this state of relaxation as often as possible, ideally once or twice daily. Even if you only take time to do this exercise once a week, you will begin to train yourself to more quickly and easily find this peaceful state of mind. This practice will, in turn, help you to find this state of calm even when you are in stressful situations.

Practice going into this state of relaxation as often as possible, ideally once or twice daily. Even if you only take time to do this exercise once a week, you will begin to train yourself to more quickly and easily find this peaceful state of mind. This practice will, in turn, help you to find this state of calm even when you are in stressful situations.

Chapter 12

Mastering Your Physiology

In chapter three we discussed both how the diva plays with your mind and how, when all else fails, you can control your inner state and find your inner strength by changing your physiology. In this chapter you will learn three exercises which will bring you into a strong physiological state. These exercises will help you remain calm, focused and aware — even when dealing with your diva.

> In this chapter you will learn three exercises which will bring you into a strong physiological state.

PRACTICE, PRACTICE, AND MORE PRACTICE

The more difficult the task the better the preparation has to be. When I prepare for a difficult concert, every note and every breath has to be planned. I've got to get the music and all of the nuances of the music into my muscles. Everything I do has to be automated and instantaneous. When great athletes train for a competition, they have to get every move into their muscles. There is no time to think about what they are doing. Their actions and reactions have to come automatically.

Just like great musicians and great athletes, the more practiced and automated your reactions to events happening around you, the better you will be at controlling your emotions. Our job in this chapter is to give you several exercises which will help you master your physiology. They will help you act and react automatically in such a way that you will remain calm, centered, and focused.

We will do this by bringing you into a strong physical state over and over again. If you find yourself tensing up, these exercises will help you recognize it and release the tension. If you find yourself getting emotionally outraged, these exercises will help you find your center again.

Apathy is denying, not dealing. It is denying that a situation may be important to you at all. This is totally different from dealing. By dealing with the situation, you know how important the situation is, you are fully aware of the consequences, and you want to succeed.

DENYING VS. DEALING – A WORD ABOUT APATHY

One thing that many of my clients have tried is to act as if they don't care. They say, "I am physically strong, and I'll stay this way, because I just don't care what happens. If the team falls apart, it falls apart." This is apathy.

Using apathy may enable you to remain emotionally detached and calm, but experience shows that if the situation is even remotely important to you, you will still be upset by it when things go wrong or conflicts occur.

Apathy is denying, not dealing. It is denying that a situation may be important to you at all. This is totally different from dealing. By dealing with the situation, you know how important the situation is, you are fully aware of the consequences, and you want to succeed. You also know that you are capable of handling it. You have a stake in the success of the situation.

If musicians or athletes choose to deal with their stress through apathy, they will not win. If they are apathetic to what happens in their concert or on the playing field, they will lack the drive and focus that they need to succeed.

Clearly, you want to succeed in the situation you are in. Otherwise you wouldn't be reading this book! Denial — apathy — is not an option.

MEDITATION AND MINDFULNESS

Although it is beyond the scope of this book to go into great detail about the many methods of meditation and mindfulness, we cannot discuss being centered and focused without touching upon the subject. Mindfulness has been proven to improve memory, focus, and cognitive flexibility.

People who practice some form of mindfulness experience much less stress, and they have the ability to react more calmly in challenging situations. In addition, they are much more flexible and find solutions more easily.

Essentially, mindfulness is a deep, moment-to-moment awareness of one's experience without judgment. In this sense, mindfulness is a state of being and not an attribute. While mindfulness may be promoted by certain practices or activities, such as meditation, it is not equivalent to or synonymous with them.

In her book, *Fully Present: The Science, Art and Practice of Mindfulness*, authors Diana Winston and Susan Smalley describe the state of mindfulness as "unentangled participation." The state of being acutely aware of what is going on around you and participating in the situation without being emotionally entangled in the situation itself.

This is our goal — that you come into a difficult situation capable of being fully present and engaged without being emotionally entangled.

Creating a state of mindfulness can be achieved through different methods. In the last chapter we saw how using mantras can help calm the mind and bring us back to the present. The mantras change our thought processes which, in turn, change our inner state.

As we saw in chapter three, you can also change your inner state through your physiology. Your physiology, or physical state, has a direct influence on your inner state, and as a result, it has a direct influence on your thought processes.

In this chapter, we will look at three exercises that will help you bring yourself into a strong, positive physical state and therefore help you remain mentally strong and flexible.

FIRST EXERCISE – DEEP BREATHING

It is no secret that breathing deeply is one of the main keys to remaining calm and centered. Deep breath exercises are found in autogenic trainings, meditation, yoga, and every form of mindfulness training available. One of the first steps in learning meditation is to breathe deeply and to concentrate on your breath.

But what exactly is a "deep breath"? As a singer, breathing deeply and calmly is essential to my craft. The voice functions through the breath, and the body reacts to every breath the singer takes. The breath determines whether or not a singer will be able to successfully sing a song — especially in classical music.

So when I ask the question, "What exactly is a 'deep breath'?" I am asking a fundamental question that in my experience is greatly misunderstood by most people. A truly deep breath is much calmer and much more passive than most people understand. In this very calm, seemingly passive deep breath, however, is a strength that is unstoppable.

Most people think that they have to physically work to breathe deeply. This could not be more wrong. Alone the concept of "having to work" puts us in a mental and physical state that is detrimental to breathing deeply. Indeed, once we are in a state of "having to work," we tighten up and attempt to cognitively control our breath. It is not possible to be centered and mindful.

> A truly deep breath is much calmer and much more passive than most people understand. In this very calm, seemingly passive deep breath, however, is a strength that is unstoppable.

So how can you easily find and implement deep breathing? In order to master breathing deeply there are two things you need to know: What exactly is a deep breath, and what causes you to physically not be able to breathe deeply.

WHAT IS A DEEP BREATH?

Just so that you can physically feel exactly what a deep breath is, do the following exercise:

Sit up straight on the front part of your chair. Close your eyes and tilt your head to the back so that your face is pointed upward toward the ceiling. Make sure that your neck remains extended without collapsing your cervical spine.

Pull your lower jaw down to the point where you feel a slight yawning sensation in the throat. Allow yourself to breathe freely and deeply through your mouth without thought or effort. In this position, your throat is open, and your breath is deep. Observe how calm and quiet your breath is. You should not hear your breathing, nor should you feel any undue tension. If you feel or hear anything, then release and relax your abdomen without collapsing the cervical spine.

Feel the chair underneath you. Feel your feet on the ground. Lay your hand on your abdomen just below your navel. Without consciously trying to control anything, especially your breathing, observe how your abdomen goes slightly outward during inhalation and slightly inward during exhalation. Be aware of your lower abdomen and let your breath be as low and deep as possible. This is your the center of your breath. Feel it expand and contract. Make sure that the upper abdominal muscles remain relaxed and released throughout the exercise. ***Just let your stomach hang.***

After breathing in and out in this posture for roughly ten to twenty breaths, bring your head forward so that you are facing straight ahead. Make sure that your breath, however, remains deep and calm. Continue to relax your abdomen and observe your breath as you quietly enjoy feeling the expansion and contraction of your lower abdomen. Enjoy being in the present.

Continue this exercise for at least three minutes concentrating on your breath. If during the exercise your thoughts begin to wander, embrace the new thoughts and release them. Return to thinking about your breath, find your center, and be in the present.

YOUR ASSIGNMENT:

Step One: Do these deep breathing exercises daily for at least six weeks, so that your body memorizes how a deep breath feels.

Step Two: Either set your cell phone alarm to randomly ring (preferably set with a rather mellow tone) five times throughout the day or set post-it notes around your office or home to remind you to breathe deeply. Every time the alarm sounds or you see one of your post-it notes, take a minute to breathe deeply. Make sure that your breath is quiet, relaxed and deep, that your abdomen just hangs. This will sharpen your awareness of how you breathe, and it trains you to immediately go into a calming, flexible posture and breathe deeply.

SELECTIVE MUSCLE RELAXATION™

In an article on emotional intelligence in the *Journal of Applied Psychology* (January 2010), Dana Joseph and Daniel Newman argue that job performance is directly related to and affected by three factors: 1) Emotion perception, or the ability to recognize or perceive which emotion you are feeling, 2) Emotion understanding, the ability to understand the emotion which you are experiencing, and 3) Emotion regulation, or the ability to control or direct an emotion in ways beneficial to you and your situation.

This research by Joseph and Newman reinforced what I had long used in my work on the operatic stage. I found that these three facets — perception, recognition, and regulation — were exactly the facets which I needed to understand and analyze in order to effectively act as well as sing on the stage.

What I mean by this is that in order to sing operatic repertoire, it is essential to remain centered and to breathe deeply. As soon as the singer becomes emotionally involved in what they are singing, the larynx lifts and the voice will often break away. This means that an operatic singer often has to decide between singing well or acting well. When faced with this decision, many singers decide that the singing is more important than the acting, and, as a result, their acting suffers. It becomes affected, unrealistic or non-existent — what we often associate with the acting in stereotypical operatic productions.

For me in my work on the stage, I did not want to have to decide between singing and acting. I loved both and wanted to do both well. In doing so, I developed the following exercise for every emotion that

Selective Muscle Relaxation™ will help you to become more acutely aware of when and how you experience different emotions. This will, in turn, help you to control them.

I had to sing: I separated the necessary physical requirements of singing from the muscular tensions that arose with each emotion I was to act.

When I began working in businesses and organizations on presence, I realized that this very exercise could be useful to help my clients better understand their emotions and help them, in turn, to remain calm, centered, and focused.

Not to be confused with Progressive Muscle Relaxation, this exercise is about recognizing and analyzing different emotions, so that you can, if you choose, maintain a positive physical state — including a deep breath — while emoting the desired emotion. This enables you to remain calm, centered, and focused regardless of the emotion you are showing in the moment. It also enables you to recognize an emotion as soon as it begins take over your body.

Emotions are not static. They have a certain progression. They begin through an impulse — most often an outside trigger, a memory, or thought process — and, if allowed, they intensify. At some point the emotional progression reaches a climax and then begins to subside.

As part of each emotion we simultaneously engage or tense up certain muscles. These muscles differ with differing emotions, although almost invariably we tighten up the upper abdomen while we experience intense emotion.

When the upper abdomen is tight, it is not possible to breathe deeply, and it is not possible to truly be calm and centered. By understanding how our body reacts to certain emotions, we can better understand how to recognize the emotion and interrupt the intensification of the emotion.

EXERCISE:

Goal: The goal of this exercise is to be able to breathe deeply despite experiencing different emotions. To be able to breathe deeply, I will ask you to release your jaw muscles, your abdomen, and your pelvic diaphragm (hips) while allowing yourself to experience different emotions. Observe what happens when you do this.

Step 1: Stand up with a relaxed posture and find your deep breath. Close your eyes.

Step 2: Imagine a situation in which you strongly feel anger (or joy, sorrow, anxiety, fear, frustration, hesitancy, loneliness, etc. Choose the emotions that you most commonly feel when dealing with your diva.)

Step 3: Let the emotion become more and more intense and allow yourself to experience the emotion with all of your senses. What do you see? What do you hear? What do you feel?

Step 4: As you do this, observe which muscles in your body tighten up or release and notice in which order the muscles contract. For example, while experiencing a situation in which you were angry, the first muscle to contract or tense up may be your jaw, then your lips, then your abdomen, then hands. This is different for each one of us. The tensions you experience and the order in which the tensions develop are unique to you. Observe these tensions and make a mental note of them.

Step 5: As you are experiencing this emotion, maintain the tensions you are experiencing everywhere, then slowly release only your jaw, abdomen, and pelvic diaphragm (hips). These muscles are key to your deep breath. As best you can, maintain the other tensions. If you tightened your arms or hands before, allow them to remain tight. While doing this make sure that you release your jaw muscles, your abdomen, and make sure that you can easily move your hips left and right. This is also much easier if you slightly tilt your head upward.

Step 6: After releasing the jaw, abdomen, and pelvic diaphragm — but while keeping other tensions (hands, arms, legs, etc.), observe what happens to the emotion you were experiencing. Has it shifted? Has it disappeared?

Step 7: Repeat the exercise with a different emotion.

This exercise will help you to become more acutely aware of when and how you experience different emotions. This will, in turn, help you to control them. You may decide if you wish to hang on to the emotion in that moment (which can sometimes be very useful) or if you wish to release your jaw, abdomen, and pelvic diaphragm so that you can breathe deeply. You become the ruler of your emotions instead of letting them rule you.

YOUR "POWER MOVE"

Have you ever wondered how musicians or athletes manage to psych themselves up before going into the game? Wouldn't it be cool to be able to get yourself into this positive state?

In this exercise, we will look at one method that musicians and athletes use to bring themselves into a strong physical and mental state: the power move (or as a Dutch colleague named it, the "Chaka!").

Imagine that you just got a phone call during which you found out that you won $5,000,000 at the lottery. How would you react?

Use your Power Move before every situation that is important to you or in which you know you will be under stress. It will give you the strength and focus you need to succeed!

Would you remain calm and cool, or would you jump up and down or run around and celebrate? Would you scream? Would you raise your arms and shout "Yeah!"? What would you do?

This sudden happy gesture — which can vary from screaming to running around to just making a fist in air — is your power move. It is a gesture unique to you, a gesture that you make when you are successful, happy, etc. Interestingly enough, these positive emotions actually get saved into the gesture itself. This means that later, if you just do the gesture, you will feel these positive emotions all over again. It is what we call an "anchor" or a "trigger." We briefly talked about these in Chapter 3.

The movement you made above (with the lottery win) is a movement that is associated with joy. Your movement may be large or small — the size of the movement is not the issue. The most important factor is how you feel inside when you do the movement.

In the case of athletes, when they win or succeed in scoring points, they usually make some sort of power move. The joy that they feel at the moment of making their gesture is anchored into the gesture. Later, if they simply do the gesture alone, all of the feelings of success and joy flow through their body as if they had just won or scored. They then use this effect to bring them into a strong physical and mental state even before the next challenge begins.

In mental training we use this anchor to make our clients emotionally strong before they go into a stressful situation. We use anchors that have been positively set to bring them into a strong physical, emotional, and mental state, so that when they are confronted with difficulties, they stay strong. As a result they are more creative, more resourceful and more successful than they would otherwise be.

EXERCISE:

Stand up and, with all of your senses, imagine the situation with the lottery. You just got the phone call. $5,000,000! It's very real! How do you react?

Observe the gestures, motion, sounds, everything about how you physically react, so that you can later replicate the physical reaction.

Every time something wonderful happens, allow yourself to physically celebrate it with your power move. Enjoy it!

Most importantly, when you know that you are about to make a difficult phone call or that you have a difficult meeting, do your

power move ahead of time to bring yourself into a strong, positive mental state. Then, after you have done your power move, make your phone call or go with confidence and assurance into your meeting!

_____

_____

_____

_____

_____

_____

Chapter 13

The Four Most Powerful Mental States

As you have experienced in these exercises, there are mental, emotional, and physical states that give you strength and make it easier for you to succeed. In this chapter I would like to walk you through the four strongest mental states, which I believe are the keys to being centered and focused, productive and creative.

These four states are the **State of Forgiveness**, the **State of Gratitude**, the **State of Play**, and the **State of Love**. As we discuss them, you will find age-old truths which may seem cliché but are important, both to your mental and emotional well-being as well as to your over-all health.

The more you choose to live your life in and aware of these four states, the stronger you will be. And you will find that problems with divas will be fewer and further between.

As we discuss the four most powerful mental states, you will find age-old truths which may seem cliché but are important, both to your mental and emotional well-being as well as to your over-all health.

THE STATE OF FORGIVENESS

It is an age-old teaching and one of the most important lessons we can learn in life: the lesson of forgiveness.

Forgiveness is both a mindset and a process, and it is by far the most valuable tool in dealing with your diva. The mindset of forgiveness is simply the willingness to forgive others unconditionally. If you hear yourself saying, "Yeah, I would forgive him/her if . . . " Then you are not in a mindset of forgiveness, you are in a mindset of conditional control. You are giving the entire control as to whether or not you are going to forgive someone to the other person. "If they do this, I will forgive them." Your forgiveness is conditional on the basis of the behavior of other person.

The mindset of forgiveness is not conditional on what the other person does. It is a conscious decision that *you* make for *yourself*. It is a highly personal decision to free yourself emotionally from the behavior of others.

This decision to be willing to forgive is the essential first step in the State of Forgiveness. Without it, the act or process of forgiveness itself becomes a chance happening. You may forgive someone simply

Forgiveness is a process. It takes time. And it is probably the most important and difficult thing for you to learn to get back to your center and concentrate on what you need.

because the thing that happened is no longer relevant or important to you. You may forgive them because your relationship is more important than the act that hurt you. In these cases forgiveness happens but not as a conscious decision on your part.

The person in a State of Forgiveness consciously says, "I choose to let go of the past and any wrongdoing that happened to me or someone I love. I choose to release the negative emotions that are holding me back and I refuse to keep reliving the past."

Forgiveness is a process. It takes time. And it is probably the most important and difficult thing for you to learn to get back to your center and concentrate on what you need.

Forgiveness is an age-old teaching and one of the most important in many faiths; and yet, few of us practice it in a constant, meaningful way. Why is that?

For one, we often believe that when we forgive, we make ourselves vulnerable to being hurt again, or we believe we will become a doormat. Another reason we find it difficult to forgive is that we equate forgiving with forgetting. But forgiving and forgetting are two completely different and separate processes. After you have chosen to forgive someone, you may end up forgetting what happened. In many cases, however, forgiveness is healthy, but remembering is essential so that mistakes will not be repeated.

WHY FORGIVE?

Forgiveness is good for your mental and physical health. Medical research in the area of forgiveness is a relatively new field. The first studies on forgiveness and health appeared in the late 1980s. Kathleen Lawler-Row, who heads up the psychology department at East Carolina University, has studied extensively the effects of both hostility and forgiveness on the body's systems.

In a 2005 study, she found that sleep quality—which has a known effect on various bodily systems—was positively correlated with forgiveness and negatively correlated with the motivation for revenge. Refusal to forgive leads to a lack of sleep which, in turn, reduces the overall health of the individual. Some typical health issues that can result directly or indirectly from not being able to forgive include high blood pressure, heart problems, stress, and burn out.

Another reason to forgive is that it frees you up to concentrate on positive things that will move *you* forward. Forgiveness is not about (or for) the other person. It's about — and for — *you*. When you forgive someone, all of the negative energy you once held in is released.

As long as we hold onto the anger, resentment, hurt, or pain we carry this person and all of the wrongdoing around with us. It is a burden that no one should have to bear. And as soon as we can forgive, the other person or the situation no longer holds us captive.

There are many books on forgiveness and many methods that different psychologist have created to help their clients learn to forgive. In my opinion, there is no one patented method to forgiveness. How an individual learns to forgive others depends on the personality of the individual involved and the situation itself.

In chapters fourteen through eighteen I will discuss how different personality structures experience forgiving, but for now it suffices to know two things:

1) The feelings of anger, hurt, and resentment are simply emotional signals that show us that we have, in some way, been wronged. They are emotions of self-preservation that help us recognize when boundaries, which should have been respected, have been crossed.

2) Although anger, hurt, and resentment show us that we have been in some way wronged, they use up a lot of energy if we hold onto them for a long period of time. In order to release those feelings and return to our center, the first step is to decide to be in a State of Forgiveness, a mindset that will allow us to release — not necessarily forget, but release — the past.

> Forgiveness is not about (or for) the other person. It's about — and for — you.

> *"The weak can never forgive. Forgiveness is the attribute of the strong."*
>
> — *Mahatma Gandhi, from All Men are Brothers: Autobiographical Reflections*

EXERCISE:

Is there a situation in which you were wronged and you are finding it difficult to forgive the others involved?

_____

_____

_____

_____

In what ways is holding onto this situation helping you?

_____

_____

_____

_____

In what ways is holding onto this situation hurting you or slowing you down?

_____

_____

_____

_____

What would you gain if you were to let go of this situation and forgive those who wronged you? (Again, we're speaking of forgiving — emotionally letting go of the situation — not necessarily forgetting.)

_____

_____

_____

_____

"Gratitude is not only the greatest of virtues, but the parent of all the others."

— Marcus Tullius Cicero, Roman Statesman and Lawyer

THE STATE OF GRATITUDE

In the last thirty years there has also been a surge of research on gratitude. As with forgiveness, living in a State of Gratitude has proven to have a positive influence on health and wellbeing. The Greater Good Science Center at University of California, Berkeley lists the physical and psychological health benefits experienced by those who consistently practice gratitude. Such benefits include:

- Having stronger immune systems and lower blood pressure
- Having higher levels of positive emotions
- Experiencing more joy, optimism, and happiness
- Acting with more generosity and compassion
- Feeling less lonely and isolated

They list gratitude as one of the most common emotions that successful people feel. Success, gratitude, and happiness go hand-in-hand and they are dependent on each other. Happiness and the ability to appreciate and enjoy success depend on gratitude.

In dealing with your diva, learning to live in a State of Gratitude will help you stay centered and focused. When you consciously choose the State of Gratitude, many challenges or problems that you have had in the past literally disappear. Your focus changes and your opportunities expand.

EXERCISE:

What are three things that you are grateful for in your life right now?

_____

_____

_____

What are three things that you are consistently grateful for on a daily basis?

_____

_____

_____

Start a gratitude journal. At the end of each day, write down what you are grateful for. Do this for thirty days and observe what changes have happened in your life.

_____

_____

_____

Success, gratitude, and happiness go hand-in-hand and they are dependent on each other. Happiness and the ability to appreciate and enjoy success depend on gratitude.

THE STATE OF PLAY

When I first saw these pictures several years ago in a TED Talk by Dr. Robert Brown, it changed my life and how I viewed communication. At that time in Germany there were several well-known trainers who taught the art of _Schlagfertigkeit_. _Schlagfertigkeit_ is a wonderful German word to describe being quick on your feet. Literally, it means "being ready to hit back." These trainers worked intensely on developing some sort of strong, often cynical comeback, which would render their opponent speechless.

Having a playful attitude enables both you and the other person to relax, open up, and begin to see the each other and the situation in a new light.

Although this type of training is not my specialty — nor is the art of attacking the other person my style — clients would often ask how I remain so *schlagfertig*, so able to defend myself when attacked. *(I often found these observations interesting, because I never felt like I was particularly good at defending myself!)*

Until I found these pictures, I really didn't have a good answer for them. We could do centering exercises and discuss different game plans, but at the end of the day, I never felt like there was a particularly good weapon they could use when they came under attack.

Then I saw these pictures. They were taken by the German photographer Norbert Rosing for the National Geographic. Norbert Rosing has specialized in photographing wild animals, in particular polar bears, and is considered to be one of the forty most influential photographers of our time.

Rosing took these pictures on the Hudson River in Canada after he and his guide, the owner of the dogs, had stopped for the evening at a kennel. There were about forty or fifty dogs at this kennel, all chained along a fence.

At about 5 p.m. they were approached by this polar bear. The polar bear was clearly hunting for food and, as you can see in the first photo, it was fixated on one of the huskies. Rosing and the guide assumed the bear would attack the husky, and although they didn't want to lose the dog, they were of the opinion that it was better the dog than them.

Photo: © Norbert Rosing, National Geographic Creative

The husky, however, did not show any fear. Instead, it went into a playful posture, going down on its front paws, wagging its tail and panting with its tongue hanging out. All physical traits that showed that the dog wanted to play.

What happened next was amazing.

Instead of attacking the dog, the bear recognized the playful posture and changed. It relaxed its fixed glare and began to play with the dogs.

Photo: © Norbert Rosing, National Geographic Creative

Photo: © Norbert Rosing, National Geographic Creative

Photo: © Norbert Rosing, National Geographic Creative

The bear even had the dog in its mouth and didn't bite it.

Photo: © Norbert Rosing, National Geographic Creative

And if you know anything about animal behavior, the most submissive posture one mammal can take is to lie on its back at the feet of another.

Photo: © Norbert Rosing, National Geographic Creative

When you genuinely want to play with the other person – full of respect and mindful awareness, not full of aggression or innuendo – there is a good chance they will also want to play with you. Barriers fall and real relationships begin to form.

The polar bear and the husky are natural enemies. The polar bear could have easily attacked the dog and stilled its hunger. And yet, when the dog went into a playful state the bear recognized this and changed its entire posture (and plans!).

These pictures showed me that when you genuinely want to play with the other person – full of respect and mindful awareness, not full of aggression or innuendo – there is a good chance they will also want to play with you. Barriers fall and real relationships begin to form.

Time and time again, this theory has proven to be true. When I know that I am about to go into a difficult situation, I just think to myself, "I want to play with you. With genuine respect and mindful awareness, I would like to play with you." It puts me into such a good state of mind, that wonderful results follow.

EXERCISE:

Do you enjoy playing sports or board games? Do enjoy going out with friends? Flirting?

Picture a situation in which you have to deal with a difficult person. As you picture it, say to yourself silently, "Full of respect and awareness, I would like to play with you." Allow yourself to relax and be playful. What happens in the situation? What changes in your attitude? What changes in the situation itself?

_____

_____

_____

_____

"Darkness cannot drive out darkness; only light can do that. Hate cannot drive out hate; only love can do that."

— Martin Luther King, Jr., Non-Violent Activist, Theologian, and Minister

THE STATE OF LOVE

The State of Love is perhaps the strongest state you can be in, and one of the most difficult to discuss in a business situation. One of the reasons that the State of Love is so challenging is because the word love means different things to different people.

One person can speak about the deep love that a parent has for a child, but if the hearer of the message comes from an abusive family, then he or she will not understand this type of love can be beautiful.

Another reason is that the word love has many facets. Love to one person may be platonic. To another, the word love would have a purely sexual meaning. Yet another person may say love is simply something invented for Hallmark cards.

To understand what I mean here by the State of Love, and to understand how this mindset can help you stay centered and focused, do the following exercise.

EXERCISE:

Take a moment to relax, and using your own understanding of the word "love," focus on someone or something that you love deeply. (Why focus on something? Some may have difficulty associating love with another person (because of abuse perhaps). Focusing on something that's important to them can help with understanding the State of Love.)

As you're doing this, allow yourself to be aware of how much you care for this person or this object or cause. How does it make you

feel? What changes in your body, in your physiology? Do you feel stronger than before? Weaker? Calmer? More excited?

_____

_____

_____

_____

Although I cannot begin to know what you are personally experiencing right now, most people, when they concentrate on someone or something they love, feel connected to something greater than themselves. A joy radiates within them. This joy and sense of belonging to something greater than yourself is a basic human need. A sense of belonging strengthens us. Being able to tap into this State of Love will give you strength and help you to find your own center.

EXERCISE ON THE FOUR STATES:

Before we explore what makes your diva tick, take a moment to think about your diva. Please imagine an unpleasant situation in which you encounter your diva. Using all five senses, allow yourself to mentally experience being with this person.

Now as you are experiencing this situation with your diva, allow your mind to think of these four states. Allow yourself to go into the State of Forgiveness: Say to yourself (while still experiencing the situation with your diva), "I am open to forgiveness. I am open to letting go of any negative emotions related to this situation or this person."

Then allow yourself to go into the State of Gratitude. Gently say to yourself (again, while still experiencing the situation with your diva), "I am grateful for so many things in life and all that life has to offer me. I am also grateful for whatever this situation may be teaching me. Gratitude and love fill my heart and mind."

And finally, allow yourself to play with your diva. Allow yourself to be light, to enjoy being with this person, to be in the State of Play.

What do you feel now? How is the situation with your diva now? Write down all that you are experiencing so you can find these feelings again when you are actually with your diva.

_____

_____

_____

_____

_____

_____

_____

_____

_____

_____

_____

_____

D
I
V
A

VALUING YOURSELF
AND YOUR DIVA

Chapter 14

How Divas Tick:
Perception, Personality, and Preferences

One of the most misunderstood things about communication is that we believe the other person should understand exactly what we mean when we say or write something. They should be able, somehow, to read our minds.

The truth is, however, the other person cannot truly know what we are thinking. And we cannot possibly know what is going on in their minds. Once we accept this fact, we begin to communicate.

As mentioned before, communication functions as bridge between two people or groups of people. In our case, we are building a bridge between you and your Diva. In the first half of this book, we concentrated on your half of the bridge. We determined what your goals are and how you can remain strong while encountering your Diva, how to make your foundation as strong as possible.

In this half of this book, we turn our attention to better understanding the Diva's side of the bridge. This will enable you to successfully connect your side of the bridge to theirs. You will learn what makes your Diva tick and how you can possibly help them create as strong a foundation as possible for their side of the bridge.

As with any bridge, both sides have their own reasons and goals for building the bridge. Each side wants to get to the other side. We've already looked at your goals. In the next chapters, we will look at the possible goals your Diva may have, what they may like to accomplish, and we will look at the common goals that you and your Diva may have. If you are on a team together, these are often your team's or organization's goals for your team.

When we build a bridge, we have to know what resources and material that each side has in order to build the bridge. Just because we have wood on our side of the river, it does not mean that they have wood on their side. In order to be stable, the bridge has to be made out of compatible materials. If they have no wood, then either we have to give them some wood for their half of the bridge or we have to build the bridge out of something else.

One of the most misunderstood things about communication is that we believe the other person should understand exactly what we mean when we say or write something. They should be able, somehow, to read our minds. In this half of this book, we turn our attention to better understanding your diva - how they think, what they may need, and how to motivate them.

Communication has three basic phases, and misunderstandings can happen at any one of these phases: the conception of the message, the transmission of the message, and the reception of the message. Miscommunications can occur during any or all of these phases.

Likewise, if they want build the bridge out of materials that we don't have, they have to supply us with some of their materials. A bridge cannot be built half out of wood and half out of concrete and be expected to be stable. Both sides have to communicate with each other to determine where, how, and when the bridge will be built. Otherwise, they will not reach their common goal.

Communication has three basic phases, and misunderstandings can happen at any one of these phases.

The first phase is the conception of the message. This phase is closely related to the person who is sending the message. This person's biases, experiences and limitations affect the message they would like to communicate. For example, a team leader is asked to send a message to their team communicating a policy, which is in conflict with the values of the team leader. This values conflict is going to affect how the team leader writes or delivers the message.

The second phase in communication is the transmission of the message. This phase has to do with both the content of the message itself and the medium used to convey the message. Let's say the team leader above decides to communicate the message by email, but the email system crashes. The message will not reach its intended recipient.

The last phase of communication is the reception of the message. This phase is closely related to the person who is intended to receive the message. The recipient is limited by his or her own experiences, value systems, and abilities. Using the example above, if the recipient of the team leader's message disagrees with the message or has strong feelings about the team leader (positive or negative), this will affect how the recipient understands and accepts the message.

There is a lot of information being thrown at us at any given moment. Our minds subconsciously filter through this information according to our belief systems, life experiences, and personality. Through these filters we extract the information we believe to be relevant. All other information is disregarded.

In order to have your message understood, to connect with and motivate the other person, and to reach your common goals, you have to understand how that person ticks. Not only that, you have to understand how you tick in comparison to that person.

This section of this book is dedicated to helping you figure out what makes people tick. We are going to look at the most important aspects of personality. We will also determine what the other person's desired outcomes are and discover how you can connect with your

Diva in such a way that their needs are met and you're both working toward your combined desired outcomes.

For the sake of simplicity, I will use three colors as a reference for describing not only the basic personality structure, but also what I call the nine PPP Traits. PPP is for Perception, Personality, and Preferences. As we go through each of the PPP Traits, I will ask you to compare each trait or tendency to that of your Diva. By recognizing which traits are stronger in you than in your Diva (and vice versa), you will begin to better understand what the other person needs.

To understand your diva better, we will look at the nine PPP traits. PPP Stands for Perception, Personality, and Preferences.

AN ANCIENT INDIAN PARABLE ON PERCEPTION

There were once six blind men who were known for being wise and clairvoyant. Their king wanted to understand the essence of the elephant, and so he ordered these wise men to find out. They were led to the animal, and were asked to reveal what they discovered.

Taking hold of the leg of the elephant, first wise man said, "Oh, the nature of this animal is clear. It is a majestic beast like the great pillars of our tallest buildings."

While holding the trunk of the elephant, the second wise man said, "No, it is like a great tree branch swaying in the air — strong and flexible, bending as it needs to."

Perplexed, the third wise man held the tail of the elephant and said, "No, my beloved colleagues, this animal is like a strong rope that holds together the four corners of our land."

Holding the ear of the elephant, the fourth wise man said, "I don't understand why you all are saying that. Clearly, this animal is like a large fan that gives us a breeze on a hot summer day."

The fifth wise man leaned against the side of the elephant and said, "I don't mean to be disrespectful, but this animal is like a great wall that protects us from our enemies."

The last of the wise men, touching the tusk of the elephant, said, "This is the most precious of materials, like the great marble from the south."

The king looked at the elephant and at his wise men and said, "You are all correct. The elephant is the most valuable animal we have. It helps us carry our burdens, fight our enemies, and gives us the precious ivory from which we can make our treasures."

This story illustrates how we, like each of the wise blind men, are influenced by our own perspective. We can only filter the information we receive through our own personal experiences.

For example, for some people their work is stressful. From their

> Different perceptions and personality traits lead to certain preferences. Just as one person may prefer email as a communication tool, another may prefer telephoning or text messages.
>
> If you understand the preferences of others, you will be able to adjust your communication style to accommodate them, and thus begin to build a strong foundation for your bridge.

perspective, someone who works a lot must have a lot of stress. Others, however, love their work, and find other aspects of life much more stressful than going to work.

As a colleague of mine once said after she managed to get her three-year-old daughter in bed, "I'd rather sing ten operas than put one child to bed!"

Everything is affected by your perspective and your perception.

PERSONALITY

Another factor we will be looking at in the next few chapters are different personality structures. Our personality structure affects how we act, think, and work. Understanding the personalities of those around you will help you understand what they need or desire and how best to communicate with and motivate them.

PREFERENCES

Different perceptions and personality traits lead to certain preferences. Just as one person may prefer email as a communication tool, another may prefer telephoning or text messages. If you understand the preferences of others, you will be able to adjust your communication style to accommodate them. As a result, you will greatly increase the chances of your Diva (or anyone else) understanding your message.

Our preferences are not simply limited to preferred communication tools; they encompass everything we do. Some people are visual learners and others are conceptual or auditory. Some people prefer to biking to work instead of walking or taking public transportation. Some people are vegetarian; others eat low-carb. Some people prefer coffee, others prefer tea.

With preferences, we simply notice the desires and tendencies of the other person, and we compare these to our own desires and tendencies.

THE NINE PERSONALITY ASPECTS

In looking at personality structures, we will specifically look at nine different aspects of the personality. These aspects are the Primary Motivator, Relationship to Others, Time Orientation, Thinking and Working, Strengths and Weaknesses, Physiological Traits and Signals, Sense of Humor, Process-Goal Orientation and the Preferred Sensory Canal.

In the next chapter we will be looking at these personality traits in greater detail, so that you can begin to understand differences in personality structures and, more importantly, differences in needs and expectations.

Let's get started!

Chapter 15

The Three "Diva" Personalities

THE THREE COMPONENTS

There are many personality analyses which help us learn more about ourselves and others. They look at different aspects of how a person reacts in different situations, and they examine inborn character traits, or the nature of the person, in comparison to learned character traits.

In my work I incorporate the Biostructure Analysis, because I find it to be the most concise and easy-to-apply analysis in everyday situations. In addition, it focuses on the inborn personality characteristics, making it more sustainable over a long period of time.

THE BIOSTRUCTURE ANALYSIS

The Biostructure Analysis, also known as the STRUCTOGRAM®, was developed by the German anthropologist Rolf W. Schirm at the end of the 1970s for a large European corporation. Schirm was asked to develop a system to help their service and sales personnel better interact with their customers and therefore improve customer satisfaction. After the service and sales personnel applied what they learned through the Biostructure Analysis, customer satisfaction rose from roughly 40% to over 90%.

The STRUCTOGRAM® is a value-free, empirical analysis which analyzes the genetically inborn personality traits that each of us have. Schirm based his extensive research on the triune brain theory from Paul MacLean, who at the time was the director of the National Institute of Mental Health in Washington, DC.

When we come into a new situation, each of us react initially from the limbic system. We determine if we are safe or if we need to either fight or flee. After this initial reaction, each of us acts and reacts to the situation differently through a complicated network of impulses in the brain. How we act and react after the initial situation is reflected in our inborn personality structure.

In my work I incorporate the Biostructure Analysis, because I find it to be the most concise and easy-to-apply analysis in everyday situations. In addition, it focuses on the inborn personality characteristics, making it more sustainable over a long period of time.

> With the Biostructure Analysis we speak of a primary dominance (the most pronounced components) and secondary dominance (the second most pronounced components).
>
> The third dominance is the weakest, or least pronounced, of the colors in our personality structure.
>
> All of us have all of these components to some degree – some more and some less.

The questions used in the Biostructure Analysis are designed to determine this inborn personality structure so that we can understand our own true nature and tendencies. This, in turn, helps us to understand what our needs are and how we can better fulfill these needs. With my clients I use the STRUCTOGRAM® to help them understand their natural tendencies and therefore be more authentic when they give a presentation. It also helps them to better understand the needs of their audience, so that they more effectively communicate their message.

In the Biostructure Analysis, we use three colors to represent the attributes given to the different parts of the triune brain. The color green represents the oldest part of the brain, the brainstem or the reptilian brain. The reptilian brain is responsible for survival and instinct. The color red represents the limbic system, which is the emotional center of the brain. The color blue represents the neocortex, which in evolutionary development is only found in primates. The neocortex allows us to plan, to create and use tools, and to think abstractly.

It is important to note that all of us have all three components; otherwise, we would be dead. This means that we all have to some degree -- some more, some less -- all of the attributes we will be looking at. The STRUCTOGRAM® is not a typology, where we can categorize individuals and therefore always predict behavior. With the STRUCTOGRAM® we observe tendencies and dominances. These tendencies and dominances give us insight into our personal nature and into our needs.

With the analysis we speak of a primary dominance (the most pronounced components) and secondary dominance (the second most pronounced components). The third dominance is the weakest, or least pronounced, of the colors in our personality structure. In some cases a person may have a so-called double dominance (where two colors are equally strong) or an evenly distributed personality structure where all three colors are equally strong.

It is also important to note that attributes like intelligence, honesty, and loyalty belong to all three colors or dominances. There is no one dominance that includes being more intelligent or more honest than another, despite what each dominance may think of themselves.

The following matrix from *Evolution of Personality* shows an overview of the three components of the Biostructure Analysis (with permission from © STRUCTOGRAM® International, IBSA Institut für Biostruktur-Analysen AG, CH-Luzern):

STRUCTOGRAM® MATRIX

	Green Component BRAINSTEM Instinctual	Red Component LIMBIC SYSTEM Emotional	Blue Component NEOCORTEX Rational
Relationship to Others	**Contact** Desire for human proximity Natural Instinct for people General popularity	**Dominance** Desire for superiority Natural authority Competitiveness	**Distance** Desire for a safe distance Naturally reserved Tendency to keep to oneself
Time Orientation	**Past** Building upon established ground Acting upon experience Avoid radical changes	**Present** Awareness of the present Impulsive action Activity and dynamism	**Future** Consideration of future consequences Planned action Striving for progress
Thinking and Working	**Getting a feel for things** Intuition and Instinct Reliable first impressions Fantasy	**Grasping ideas** Decisive thinking Rapid recognition of feasibility Tendency to improvise	**Orderliness** Systematic thought Highly perceptive thinking Tendency for perfection
Success based on . . .	Popularity and Empathy	Inspiring enthusiasm in others	Convincing others through data and facts

© STRUCTOGRAM® International, IBSA Institut für Biostruktur-Analysen AG, CH-Luzern

THREE DIVA PERSONALITIES

For our purposes here, we will not be doing the Biostructure Analysis, simply because it is not possible to do without the personal support of a licensed, trained instructor. In the endnotes I have listed the contact information of the international STRUCTOGRAM® Center where you can get further information about seminars and trainers in your area that offer this highly effective analysis, or contact my office for further information.

Many of the truths found in the analysis, however, will help you understand your Diva better. Again, every one of us has all of the personality traits that we are about to discuss to a more or less degree. Using the nine personality aspects mentioned in the last chapter, we will look at how a person would be if they had the most extreme personality traits of each of the three components. These are the three Diva personalities.

Know thyself.

— Gnothi seauton

THE PEOPLE'S PERSON DIVA

Have you ever met someone who tends to arrive late to meetings and seems somewhat chaotic? You may be in contact with a People's Person Diva! The People's Person Diva is — as the name implies — a people's person. They tend to be rather chaotic, creative, and show an immediate interest in others. They have a strong need for harmony and will try to keep the peace at all costs.

The People's Person Diva is primarily motivated by developing relationships and connecting with others.

PRIMARY MOTIVATOR: PEOPLE AND RELATIONSHIPS

The **People's Person Diva** is primarily motivated by **developing relationships and connecting with others.** This person has an excellent understanding of human nature and builds trusting relationships quickly. They have a strong desire for harmony and are therefore willing to compromise to keep peace. When deciding to buy a product, for example, the People's Person Diva will often base their decision on how close their relationship to the sales person is.

RELATIONSHIP TO OTHERS: CONTACT

The **People's Person Diva** desires **human proximity**. They find isolation difficult. They believe that sharing their troubles eases the burden and sharing their joys increases happiness.

The People's Person Diva has a natural instinct for people. The larger this component, the livelier their interest is in other people and their lives. The People's Person Diva gets along easily and well with others and contact to others is uncomplicated and spontaneous. People tend to trust the People's Person Diva from the minute they meet, and they are often inclined to rather quickly open up to the People's Person Diva telling them secrets that they would not normally share with people they don't know.

Because of this love of human contact and the genuine interest in others, the People's Person Diva is generally popular. They are often gregarious and empathetic in nature and trust comes naturally.

TIME ORIENTATION: PAST

The **People's Person Diva** is oriented in the **past**. The "good old days" or "how it used to be" might be common phrases used by a People's Person Diva. They tend to be traditional and conservative, and they prefer to build upon established ideas and traditions. Memories are of great importance, and they dislike parting with souvenirs of the past. They are often collectors or messies.

The stronger this tendency is, the less likely the People's Person Diva is going like or accept change. They prefer not to experiment. The desire to begin a new life, move to a new country, or pioneer in any field is far less strong in a People's Person Diva than in our other two diva types.

THINKING AND WORKING: INSTINCTIVE

The **People's Person Diva** is **highly instinctive and has a strong intuition.** We all have a huge reservoir of subconsciously recorded experience. The People's Person Diva has the ability to tap into this potential resource and consciously act upon it. This is what we know as instinct, and it can lead to reliable, intuitive judgement. The People's Person Diva's first impressions of other people and situations tends to be very reliable, and they have the subconscious gift of sensing and interpreting signals given out by others.

The People's Person Diva is very creative and imaginative. They tend to see the "big picture" in the creative process, although they often easily lose touch with reality.

STRENGTHS AND WEAKNESSES

The **People's Person Diva** is highly **instinctive**. They have an excellent understanding of human behavior and their gut reactions about new situations are usually accurate. The People's Person Diva emotes a caring attitude, which causes others to trust them rather quickly. Even animals sense the kindness of the People's Person Diva and often try to interact with them. The People's Person Diva's successes are based on the fact that they are well liked and trusted.

It is often difficult for the People's Person Diva to recognize that other people may need more personal space and may not like such close contact. In addition, the People's Person Diva tends to be chaotic. This chaos, the tendency to arrive at planned meetings late, and the tendency to talk way more than necessary are the main weaknesses that a People's Person Diva brings to the table.

PHYSIOLOGICAL SIGNALS: SYMPATHETIC

The **People's Person Diva** tends to use relatively few, **small gestures**, but they have a very expressive face. Through these facial expressions, you can easily see what a People's Person Diva is thinking. When a People's Person Diva enters a room full of people, they stay briefly in the doorway and look around for familiar faces. Then they join those they already know, or those who appear most sympathetic. The People's Person Diva is not interested in being the life of the party, but they do want to get to know the people there.

SENSE OF HUMOR: SELF-DEPRECATING

The **People's Person Diva** is most likely to make **cute, self-deprecating jokes** or jokes about common characteristics that we all share.

PROCESS-GOAL ORIENTATION: CAN BE EITHER

The **People's Person Diva** can be either **goal-oriented or process-oriented**, depending on how strong other personality traits are.

"This above all: to thine own self be true, And it must follow, as the night the day, Thou canst not then be false to any man."

— *William Shakespeare, Polonius' Monologue to Laertes from The Tragedy of Hamlet, Prince of Denmark*

PREFERRED SENSORY CANAL: AUDITORY

The **People's Person Diva** can most easily retain information through the **auditory** canal.

THE DOMINANT DIVA

The Dominant Diva is predominantly motivated by power and dominance.

Have you ever known anyone who owns the room as soon as they enter? They exude an energy so strong that you literally feel them coming into the room? If you have, then you were most likely encountering a person with strong Dominant Diva tendencies.

PRIMARY MOTIVATOR: COMPETITION

The **Dominant Diva** is predominantly motivated by **power and dominance**. When a Dominant Diva enters the room, they size up the other people in the room and decide who is in charge. Once that is determined, they decide whether or not they have a chance of being the leader. If yes, they begin to take control of the situation.

RELATIONSHIP TO OTHERS: DOMINANCE

The **Dominant Diva** wants to be the **alpha dog in social relationships**. This person is often the decision maker in the crowd and is usually the first to take the initiative, especially in critical situations. Conversation is straight-forward and direct, and colleagues or partners are often seen as sources of comparison and rivalry. Competition is a challenge which they take on or even actively seek in order to prove their dominance.

The **Dominant Diva** also has a **natural authority**. The larger the red component, the more they are recognized and respected by others, even if they do not consciously seek this recognition. Status symbols are also important to the Dominant Diva. For example, if a Dominant Diva has money, they will buy the most expensive, newest car. If the Dominant Diva doesn't have money, they will get a car which stands out some other way. They like to be unique.

TIME ORIENTATION: PRESENT

The **Dominant Diva** lives in the **present**, in the here and now. He has a "just do it" attitude. They are not interested in the past and not overly concerned about the future.

THINKING AND WORKING: GRASPING OF IDEAS, PRAGMATIC

The **Dominant Diva** is a **"hands on"** type of person. "Just do it," "just try it out" are typical for the Dominant Diva mentality.

In addition, the Dominant Diva is highly pragmatic. They can look at a situation and assess the practicality and do-ability of the situation almost instantly. The Dominant Diva is spontaneous and thinks fast on their feet. They like to improvise. Often, in an emergency, the Dominant Diva is the first person to react.

STRENGTHS AND WEAKNESSES

The **Dominant Diva's** primary strengths are their **charisma** and their ability to **motivate others**. They are natural leaders.

On the down side, the **Dominant Diva** tends to **run over others** emotionally or physically. They lose their temper easily and tend to be rash in making decisions. Those decisions are often forgotten or changed as soon as the situation changes. "Why would I be interested in what I said or what we decided yesterday? Today is a new day!"

PHYSIOLOGICAL SIGNALS: LARGER THAN LIFE

The **Dominant Diva** tends to use **large gestures and few facial expressions.** The Dominant Diva's voice tends to be loud and somewhat pressed. When they enter a room full of people, they fill the room with their energy, and they immediately become the center of attention.

SENSE OF HUMOR: DEROGATORY

The **Dominant Diva** tends to have a sense of humor that **makes fun of a group or race of people** in order to show dominance and supremacy.

PROCESS-GOAL ORIENTATION: GOAL

The **Dominant Diva** is highly **goal-oriented.** The end justifies the means. This orientation gives the Dominant Diva a strong focus and the ability to motivate others towards the goal. On the down side, in their pursuit of the goal, they may run over everything and everyone in their path.

PREFERRED SENSORY CANAL: KINESTHETIC

The **Dominant Diva** is **kinesthetic**. This means that they need movement to be able to concentrate or focus. Being locked in a room without being able to move is one of the worst things that can happen to a Dominant Diva. This means that in order to learn information and make decisions the Dominant Diva should be able to walk around and freely move their body.

The **Planner Diva** is motivated by the pursuit of **perfection**.

THE PLANNER DIVA

The last Diva that we will be looking at is the Planner Diva. The Planner Diva is more introverted and quiet, in many ways the opposite of the Dominant Diva.

PRIMARY MOTIVATOR: PERFECTION

The **Planner Diva** is motivated by the pursuit of **perfection**. They want to know that all of the information, facts, and data have been collected before they make a decision. The Planner Diva is focused on the future and is always striving to improve whatever they are working on.

RELATIONSHIP TO OTHERS: DISTANCE

The **Planner Diva** has a desire for **distance** between themselves and another person. The Planner Diva has an aversion to getting too close to other people and strongly dislikes other people getting too close to them, especially initially in a relationship.

The Planner Diva is reserved, especially in new situations. It takes them longer to warm up to people, especially when the environment is not conducive. The Planner Diva rarely hits it off with others immediately and tends to make a better impression over the course of time.

The Planner Diva has a tendency to not show emotions. The Planner Diva is sensitive and experiences profound emotions, but they keep them to themselves. The Planner Diva often seems cool, somewhat arrogant, and difficult to fathom.

TIME ORIENTATION: FUTURE

The **Planner Diva** is a **planner**. They think predominantly in the **future**. "How can we improve this?" or, "What will happen if or when we…?" are common to the thought processes of the Planner Diva. They are not particularly interested in what is now or what was in the past, but in what is possible in the future.

The Planner Diva does not like spontaneity and usually arrives early to meetings and events.

THINKING AND WORKING: ORDERLINESS

The **Planner Diva** strives toward **order and orderliness**. The larger the blue component, the more systematic the person thinks and the better they are able to see interrelationships and structures in apparently unordered data. The Planner Diva has an inquisitive desire to get to the bottom of things.

The Planner Diva is also highly perceptive. The larger this trait is, the greater the tendency for abstract thinking. They can often master abstract codes more readily than direct communication through the spoken word, body language, or visual images.

The Planner Diva has a strong tendency towards perfection, and they prefer the written language over spoken language. They are not satisfied with the "gist" of things; they prefer to find precisely the right word to express what they wish to communicate.

STRENGTHS AND WEAKNESSES

The primary strengths of the **Planner Diva** are their **perfectionism** and their **reliability**. The Planner Diva double and triple checks their facts to make sure that the information collected is correct and covers all possible scenarios. The main reasons for the success of a Planner Diva is their ability to convince others through rational argument.

The greatest risk for the Planner Diva is the strong tendency toward **perfectionism**. This can often delay the completion of their tasks. The careful consideration of all alternatives and the wish to exclude all elements of risk makes it difficult for the Planner Diva to make decisions. In addition, the desire to work alone and keep distant from others can lead to isolation from possible useful collaborators.

PHYSIOLOGICAL SIGNALS: RESERVED

When a **Planner Diva** enters a room, they tend to stay **closer to the door**, more on the edge of the crowd instead of being the center of attention. The Planner Diva would rather be alone and doesn't enjoy making idle small talk. The Planner Diva tends to use few, relatively small gestures and few facial expressions.

SENSE OF HUMOR: CALCULATED

Political satire, complicated reasoning, and word-play are typical for the **Planner Diva's** sense of humor. The Planner Diva's jokes tend to be well thought-out and calculated.

PROCESS-GOAL ORIENTATION: PROCESS

The **Planner Diva** is very **process** oriented. The down side of this is that the Planner Diva will often tend to get lost in the details of the process and lose sight of the goal.

PREFERRED SENSORY CANAL: VISUAL

The **Planner Diva** tends to prefer the **visual** canal. In order to comprehend something, they prefer to see it on paper or in writing. Also, the Planner Diva likes orderliness. Too much chaos or too many gestures from another person can be highly distracting for the Planner Diva.

_____

_____

_____

_____

_____

_____

_____

_____

Chapter 16

So, You Think You Know Your Diva?

Now that we have gone through this overview of the three divas, let us see how well you can recognize what possibly motivates your diva. Again, remember that all of us have elements of all three divas in us, and these influence each of us differently. Your job is to observe which tendencies are stronger in your diva than in you.

Here is a small challenge for you:

THE CHALLENGE

Person A works on a team with twelve other people. As team leader you notice that over time Person A has been taking over the responsibilities of other team members. Finally, one day in the weekly team meeting Person A says, "I can't take it anymore! I have to do everything myself, and no one is helping!"

The dangers from this type of behavior are many. Not only might the person involved become burnt-out, but the other members of the team may become less motivated. When one person takes over the responsibilities of the others, a rather clear message is communicated: "I don't think you are capable of handling this task as well as I would."

This communicated message is dangerous because once doubt at any level is brought into the equation, people lose motivation and often become resentful, possibly even rebellious.

So, given this information, what type of diva is Person A? And how can you help your team to get back on track?

The answer: It depends.

Before reading any further, how would you go about finding out what Diva personality structures may be involved?

_____

_____

_____

_____

To order to recognize the true motivations another person, it is essential that you observe them in many different situations.

The tendency to take over the tasks of other people can happen with all three divas. The difference between the three is the motivation behind the person doing it.

A **People's Person Diva** wants to help others. They see that the others are having difficulty or are getting behind, and they want to come to the rescue.

A **Dominant Diva** wants either wants to call attention to themselves as being the team's savior, or they want to get the task done as soon as possible.

A **Planner Diva** will tend to take over the responsibilities of another person, because their perfectionist tendencies cause them to believe that others will not do the work as thoroughly and accurately as they would. They firmly believe that they are the only person capable of administering this task, and if it is given to someone else, mistakes will be made.

RECOGNIZING TRUE MOTIVATIONS

To begin to recognize the true motivations of Person A, it is essential that you observe them in more situations than just this one. If you have observed that they are a process-oriented perfectionist who constantly tries to find better solutions to problems, then you won't be surprised when they say they just want the task to be done correctly. This person will need help letting go and letting others learn, even if the others make mistakes.

If you have observed that Person A is a people person, somewhat chaotic and chatty, then it won't be surprising to observe that they simply want to help their teammates. In this case Person A will have to be reassured that you believe firmly that their teammates are fully capable of getting the job done, and that by taking the jobs away they may be doing more harm than good.

If you have observed that Person A is dynamic, charismatic, spontaneous, and energetic, then observe if the person tends to take over meetings or put himself in the spotlight. If this is the case, Person A may well be a Dominant Diva and as a result may want to be the alpha dog. It can also be that Person A may want a promotion, or they may just be impatient and want the project to move forward.

HELPING OTHER TEAM MEMBERS GET THEIR RESPONSIBILITIES BACK

Depending on the motivation behind the team take-over, getting the team back on track will take a deep understanding of the situation. Let's look at each of the dominances and possible strategies to help solve the situation.

In all of these situations, it is important that you establish your-self as team leader. This means that your team knows that you are there for them *and for Person A*. Often I have observed situations where a team leader prematurely believes that they have to side either with the team or with Person A, defending the behavior of one or the other. In most cases this is not necessary. As team leader you have the responsibility to remain neutral and to get your team back on track, preferably with the team remaining intact.

IF PERSON A IS PLANNER DIVA

If Person A is a Planner Diva — again, there is a difference in how strong this component may be — their tendency will be to strive toward perfection. The Planner Diva will take over the tasks of other team members if they are of the opinion that the others are not doing their work well enough. Person A is convinced that they are the only one in the group who will carry out the tasks meticulously and thor-oughly enough to reach the team's goal.

Person A will often appear arrogant and demeaning to the team. If there are other Planner Divas on the team, they may understand why Person A is acting this way, but — especially if they are also targeted — most team members will be insulted by the implication from Person A that their work is not accurate and thorough enough.

Your job as team leader is to communicate to the team that you know they are not only more than capable of thoroughly and accu-rately accomplishing their tasks, but that the synergy of teams who work together has been proven to be far more creative, productive, and sustainable than a team of one (or a team where one person does everything).

A classical example of this was the discovery of DNA. Although Francis Crick and James Watson ultimately discovered the double helix model for DNA, they were initially far behind a more brilliant researcher, Rosalind Franklin.

Franklin worked together with Maurice Wilkins and Raymond Gosling on developing a model for DNA, but because she was such a difficult person to work with and had a tendency to go off on her own, Wilkins described her as having "an air of cool superiority." They did not make as much progress as Crick and Watson. At the end of the day, they lost the race to define DNA to Crick and Watson because of their lack of ability to work together.

If Person A is a Planner Diva — again, there is a difference in how strong this component may be — their tendency will be to strive toward perfection.

If your Planner Diva truly wants the team to succeed, then it is essential that the team members work together toward the goal.

IF PERSON A IS A PEOPLE'S PERSON DIVA

> If Person A is a People's Person Diva, they are creative, somewhat chaotic, and have a strong desire for harmony.

If Person A is a People's Person Diva, they are creative, somewhat chaotic, and have a strong desire for harmony. This person wants to make sure that everyone in the group is happy. The People's Person Diva also wants to establish personal relationships with the others in the group, and to some extent feels responsible for the others. In addition, the People's Person Diva has difficulties saying, "No."

When a People's Person Diva takes on the tasks of other team members, it is to help them out and to support them. Persuading them to stop helping others by taking over their tasks may be most difficult of all three divas, because the reason is altruistic, and they will maintain that they are fine with the work overload. The additional burden is not too much for them.

It is helpful to explain to the People's Person Diva that the team will be stronger when tasks are shared by all team members, and by taking over the tasks of the others, they are subconsciously communicating that others are less competent and capable of successfully completing the tasks. The tasks should be returned to the original owner, preferably with the sentence, "I've been working on this for some time now, and I genuinely believe that you would do it better than I."

IF PERSON A IS A DOMINANT DIVA

> The Dominant Diva takes over the tasks of other people primarily for one of two reasons: either the team is not moving fast enough for them or they are strategically calculating a way to dominate the team or the project.

One of the more challenging situations is when the Person A is Dominant Diva. Their motivation is usually to further their own interests or to be in control. The Dominant Diva takes over the tasks of other people primarily for one of two reasons: either the team is not moving fast enough for them or they are strategically calculating a way to dominate the team or the project.

The easiest way to find out which of these two motivations is at play is simply to ask how they think things are going. If the main complaint or concern is that everything is going too slowly, then it is most likely impatience that is motivating them. Since the Dominant Diva is goal-oriented, they would like to have the project done yesterday. In this case, it is important to explain to them that you understand and appreciate their desire to get everything done as quickly as possible, but it is not good for the team if the others are not involved in the process.

More complicated is the situation when the person wants to be in charge or to dominate everyone. This is complicated because they'll hide their true motivation behind trying to be helpful.

"Oh, you're so busy, I can do that for you."

It seems harmless and helpful at first, but if it is part of a desire to take over everything, the team may genuinely be in danger. This person may even have their sights on the team leader position or higher up, and they may be strategically trying to undermine the success of others to put themselves on top.

If this is the motivation of your colleague, carefully observe what is going on and stop the process of their taking over other people's responsibilities. First speak to the other teammates and ask them to not give up any further work. Then you should talk to the Dominant Diva about their goals and desires, what they would like to be doing in the company and elsewhere in ten years. This will begin to show you if their motivations are a subtle takeover. With this information you may be able to help them reach their goals without letting the team suffer under their ambitions.

BACK TO YOUR DIVA

Now that we have looked more closely at the different dominances and how they reveal themselves in certain situations, reflect on your situation.

From this example, analyze your situation with your Diva. Do you recognize certain tendencies? What might their personality structure be? Given this information, how could you possibly better communicate with your Diva? What might be some of their needs or desires?

Often it is easier to recognize the personality structure of another person through a comparison to your own tendencies. For example, who arrives first (a Planner Diva element)? Who is more distant during the conversation (Planner Diva element)? Who is livelier (a Dominant or People's Person Diva element)? Who is more willing to compromise (People's Person Diva element)? Who needs more information (Planner Diva element? Who makes fast decisions (Dominant Diva element)? Find a partner and observe their behavior in comparison to yours, and write down your observations — both of yourself and your partner.

_____

_____

_____

_____

_____

_____

_____

_____

_____

Chapter 17

The Diva's Desired Outcome

Now that we have begun to look at what the tendencies and desires of your diva might be, we will use this information to look at their possible goals and motivations. If you surmise, for example, that your diva has a strong blue element, then it is possible that their desire is to plan better or collect more information.

One of the most common communication mistakes, especially with persons in leadership positions, is to dictate our desired goals and to assume that these will automatically be the goals of every member of our team. We tend to think we know best or that these goals are obvious.

You may try to tell others what you think their goals should be, but if they do not see their own advantage in what you propose, they will not begin to accept your goal as their own. It remains *your* goal for them, not their goal for themselves. They may even make a point of taking the opposite point of view simply to prove you wrong. Understanding your diva's goals will not only help you know them better, it will help them become better team members.

I often hear that the goal should be absolutely clear: to get the job done! It is rarely, however, as clear as we think!

> One of the most common communication mistakes, especially with persons in leadership positions, is to dictate our desired goals and to assume that these will automatically be the goals of every member of our team. We tend to think we know best or that these goals are obvious.

THE ADVANTAGES TO UNDERSTANDING THEIR GOALS AND DESIRED OUTCOMES

There are many advantages to finding out the goals and desired outcomes of the other person. First, it helps you to gauge how close you may be to finding common ground and improving communication with this person. Second, it helps you to develop your strategy in dealing with this person. Once you know what they desire, you will better understand them and that which motivates them. These two elements are key to employee satisfaction and engagement.

KNOWING THEIR GOALS CHANGES EVERYTHING!

Eric, a physician, came to me several years ago to ask for help in preparing himself for a difficult meeting. His contract with the

Appearing self-confident, competent, and intelligent is superficial. *Being* self-confident, competent, and intelligent has to do with two factors: 1) having full knowledge of your strengths and resources and 2) having an effective strategy to communicate these.

hospital was due to expire in two months, and neither his boss nor the hospital administration had indicated whether or not his contract would be extended. He knew he had to broach the situation with his boss — someone he considered to be distant and uninterested in him — and ask for an extension of his contract.

Eric's contract until this point had been limited to two years, because with a limited contract, the hospital could keep his salary at the lowest possible rate. This two-year contract had already been renewed once, and Eric wanted some guarantee that his position was secure, and that he finally would receive some cost of living increase. He did not want to go another two years wondering whether or not he would have to uproot himself and his family to find another position.

I asked him if this meeting were to go well, what would be the desired result? What were his personal goals for this meeting?

Obviously, Eric said that he wanted his contract renewed and some guarantee that his position was secure. He then went on to say that what he really wanted was to receive tenure, and he wanted his boss to recognize that he was a valuable member of the hospital staff.

When I asked him what I could do for him, he answered that he wanted me to help him prepare for this talk so that he would appear self-confident, competent, intelligent and worthy of tenure.

Appearing self-confident, competent, and intelligent is superficial. *Being* self-confident, competent, and intelligent has to do with two factors: 1) having full knowledge of your strengths and resources and 2) having an effective strategy to communicate these.

Although it was clear to me that Eric had all of the skills necessary to be successful in this meeting, he had too much self-doubt and no effective strategy to successfully convince his boss he was necessary to the everyday function of the hospital.

We began the coaching with helping Eric connect to his own resources. We brought to the forefront of his conscious mind his skills, talents, commitment, his love for his patients, and his talent for leading his team. Then we did the Meta-Position game, an exercise I will discuss in further detail.

In the Meta-Position game, Eric was asked to observe and analyze from different perspectives the conversation he was going to have with his boss. In this process, he discovered that his personal goals were quite different from his boss's personal goals.

Eric began the exercise by placing himself in his role on the day of his meeting with his boss. He entered his boss's office and began the conversation by saying that his contract was about to expire, and he needed to know if it would be extended.

As he put himself in the role of his boss, he realized that his boss really didn't want to be bothered with this contract. The only thing that really interested his boss was the research that his team was doing. I asked Eric if he had anything to do with that research, and he answered, "Yes, I lead the team."

When Eric put himself into the Meta Position, the position of the observer, he observed that the conversation would be more effective if Eric were to start with that which interests his boss (the research) and then mentioned his contract afterwards.

When the day came, here is what happened: Eric enters his boss's office and says, "I just want to bring you up to date on our research..." After he gives his boss this update, he says, "Oh, and by the way, my contract ends next month."

His boss is shocked! "How can the person who is leading my research team have a limited contract?!" At the end of the day, by understanding his boss's personal goals and desired outcomes, Eric was able to obtain not only tenure, but also a substantial raise in salary and over a short period of time, a rather nice promotion. This all happened simply because he took the time to understand the personal goals and desires of the other person.

THE META-POSITION GAME

The Meta-Position game is one of the best ways I have found to help my clients discover what the other person's goals and desires might be. Pick a situation in which you will be encountering your diva. It can be a situation out of the past that has already happened, or it can be a situation that will be happening in the future. Pick a situation that is causing you stress and that will help you better understand how your diva ticks.

GETTING STARTED

The first step in the Meta-Position game is to take three pieces of paper. On one piece of paper write "Position 1." On the second piece of paper write "Position 2," and on the third piece of paper, write "Meta-Position." Place these three pieces of paper on the ground in a triangle as seen here:

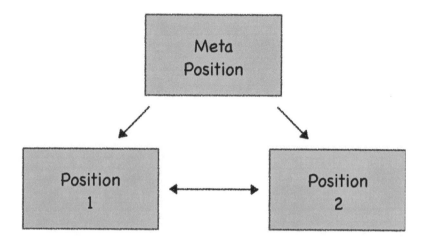

Position 1 is you. Everything you do and observe from this position is from your perspective.

Position 2 is the other person. It can also be a group of people. When you stand on the "Position 2" piece of paper, everything you do or observe is from the perspective of the other person.

The Meta-Position is the observer. When you stand on this position, you are no one. You are neutral. You have the ability to observe the situation and the people involved without emotional attachment.

PLAYING THE GAME

Step 1: Write down five of your strengths. These can be personality traits or skills you have learned over the years. (enthusiasm, curiosity, love for your work, ability to communicate, etc.)

Step 2: Define the situation you are about to work on and what your desired outcome is.

Step 3: Step onto the paper "Position 1" and describe the situation out loud — this is important — from before you enter the situation and encounter the other person(s) to the end of the encounter.

As you put yourself in the role of yourself in the situation, use all of your senses. Allow the situation to progress in time, and as it progresses, at each step of the encounter, answer the following questions:

- What do you see?
- What do you hear?
- What to feel?
- What do you smell or taste?

Step 4: After you have thoroughly described the situation from your perspective, step onto the "Position 2" paper. From here, describe the situation from the perspective of the other person.

Again, use all of your senses to describe the situation as it progresses. What do you see, hear, feel etc.? Be careful only to observe the situation from their perspective and always use the pronoun "I" or "we," because in this position you are the other person. Also, take into consideration what you have learned about personality structures and needs. What might you, as this person, need or desire?

Step 5: After you have gone through the entire situation in the second position, step onto the "Meta-Position" paper. From here you are the neutral observer.

As the neutral observer — and please be as critical as possible from this position — observe Position 1 and Position 2 as they have this encounter. What do you see? What do you hear? How are the body languages of both parties? How well are they communicating with each other? What could be improved to better the communication between the two?

Take your time with this position, because this position will give insight into things you cannot otherwise observe. From this position, give the person in Position 1 advice about how to improve the situation. (We can only give Position 1 advice, because the real Position 2 is someone whose behavior we cannot change. We can only modify our behavior and understanding of the situation, and observe how this affects the entire encounter.)

Step 6: Step outside of the triangle, and consider what resources you may need to better communicate with Position 2. Use the list you made in Step 1 to assist you with this.

What other resources do you have that you might have not have thought about earlier but may be helpful in this situation? Skills? Values? Relationships?

Step 7: Taking the advice that you were given by the Meta-Position and using the resources you have available to you, step onto the Position 1 paper again.

Using the advice and resources, change your behavior to improve the encounter. Again, go chronologically through the situation, including how you plan to act and what you plan to say, and observe the situation with all of your senses.

Step 8: Step onto the Position 2 paper and go through the situation again. What has changed? How is this different than the first round?

Step 9: Step onto the Meta-Position paper and observe the conversation again. What has changed? Is it better than before? Will these changes lead to both Position 1 and 2 reaching their goals? Does anything else need to be changed or improved?

Step 10: Repeat the entire process from Step 2 as often as necessary to create your game plan for your encounter with your diva.

_____

_____

_____

_____

_____

_____

_____

_____

Chapter 18

Your Common Desired Outcome

In the course of this book, we've defined the situations in which you encounter your diva. We've talked about strategies on how to help you stay calm, centered, and focused. We've discussed how to better understand your diva and to build a bridge to your diva so that you can reach your goals and help them reach their goals, so that you can create a win-win situation.

At the heart of all of this is the situation in which you have been thrown into together with your diva, your workplace, your team, etc. And as part of this situation, there is often a common goal or a common desired outcome.

For some of you, you are not having to work closely together every day with your diva to accomplish some joint goal. For you, this chapter may be less relevant. If, however, you are regularly thrown together into situations with your diva, please do read on. Something (workplace, team, project, etc.) is bringing you together with this person, and it is worth taking a look at the situation to see if there just might be a common desired outcome, something that is greater than the two of you.

There are two types of common goals or desired outcomes that I would like to look at with you here. The first is the true purpose of your team, your business or your organization, what I call your "Music." The second type of common goal is the concrete goal that your team has to accomplish right now in this particular situation.

> There are two types of common goals or desired outcomes that I would like to look at with you here. The first is the true purpose of your team, your business or your organization, what I call your "Music."

WHAT IS YOUR "MUSIC"?

When musicians come together to make music, we have one goal: to serve the music. Yes, it is easier and more fun to make music when we love all of the musicians with whom we're working, but this is often not the case. One thing holds true: regardless of any personal disputes, we know that there is one thing that is greater than every one of us. The one thing that bonds us together and creates art: the music.

In theater, the show must go on. All of the actors, singers, dancers, musicians, stage crew, and tech are there to serve the show. They are there to create a fantasy world for the audience that can only be created when everyone pulls together. Does this mean that everyone working on the show gets along great with everyone else? No, they rarely do! But the show must go on. The show takes precedent over everything. All decisions are reached according to how they enhance the theater experience for the audience. Is the show served by adding this element or not. If not, the element is not included.

My question for you: What is your music? Who or what are you there to serve?

In a hospital or in a doctor's office, staff who do not get along with each other should never allow this conflict to be sensed by a patient. They are there to serve the patient, to help the patient in every way possible to have a healthy and speedy recovery. The patient is their "music." Staff who argue in front of the patient or speak badly about others in front of the patient are affecting the experience that the patient is having, and through this, they are affecting the patient's recovery.

How would you feel if two actors were in the middle of a love scene on stage, and suddenly one of the two actors breaks out of character and refuses to kiss the other actor simply because he doesn't like her (or she doesn't like him) in real life? As an audience member you would not accept it. You would want your money back for the ticket you bought, and you would be right!

How would you feel if two musicians began arguing in the middle of a concert and didn't finish the composition? The hospital is no different. Your business, your organization is no different. We are all part of something greater than ourselves, and this thing — whatever or whomever it may be — is your music. You and your team are there to serve it.

EXERCISE

In your situation with your diva, are you part of a larger organization? If so, whom or what do you serve? What might your "music" be?

_____

_____

_____

Does everyone clearly agree that this is your "music"? Or are there differing opinions as to what or whom your organization serves?

_____

_____

_____

If there are differing opinions about this, what are possible sources of the differing opinions? How can the leadership in your organization bring everyone together onto the "same page," so to speak? How can the organization better communicate its sense of purpose?

_____

_____

_____

GETTING THE JOB DONE

Many of you have regular contact with your diva. For some of you, this contact may be weekly or even daily. You work on a team with them, and your team has real outcomes that it has to accomplish. You have to "get the job done," whatever that may be. Your organization is counting on you.

These outcomes are the common goals that both you and your diva share, and they are for the good of the organization. You may be working on long-term goals or short-term goals. You may be developing a product, or you may provide a service for customers or for your organization. Your goals may be ongoing or they may be part of a one-time project that will first be realized in many months or perhaps even years.

These are the goals that bind your team together and give it purpose. These are also the specific goals that connect you and your team to your organization. These goals should be shared, understood and mutually agreed upon by all parties.

In your situation with your diva, what are some of the concrete goals that you may have in common? Are they a one-time project or are they recurring? If you were to say, "We should just get it done!" What is the "it"?

_____

_____

_____

The second type of common goal is the concrete goal that your team has to accomplish right now in this particular situation. These are the goals that bind your team together and give it purpose. These are also the specific goals that connect you and your team to your organization. These goals should be shared, understood and mutually agreed upon by all parties.

> Does every member of your team understand the importance of their role in accomplishing these goals, or do you have people on your team that think that their talents or services are irrelevant?

Once this desired outcome has been articulated, look at all the possible challenges that may hinder achieving this goal. Using the many techniques that we have looked at in this book, observe what elements may be holding your team back. Are there communication challenges which have not yet been addressed? Are there personality challenges which still may stand in the way of your success? Is everyone "on board" with the established goals?

_____

_____

_____

Does everyone on your team share the opinion that these goals are the set goals for your team, or do you have differing opinions about what you are supposed to accomplish?

_____

_____

_____

Does everyone on your team understand exactly what these goals are, and can they verbalize both the desired outcomes and what their role is in accomplishing these outcomes?

_____

_____

_____

Does every member of your team understand the importance of their role in accomplishing these goals, or do you have people on your team that think that their talents or services are irrelevant?

This question is important for everyone on the team to answer — not only about themselves, but about the other members of the team as well — because only when we understand how important each team member is can we show each team member the respect they deserve. And only when we understand how important our own role is — no matter how large or small — can we fully support the team in a meaningful way.

Take, for example, my absolute favorite symphony, Dvorak's 9th Symphony, "From the New World." One of my favorite moments in this symphony is a passage in the fourth movement where the brass and wind instruments carry the main theme and the strings vacillate between echoing this theme and playing small interjected passages.

At first glimpse the strings don't really seem that important. They don't play the main theme except to copy it from the others. Really they only play little short scales that in and of themselves don't seem to be relevant at all. Yet, these seemingly irrelevant passages are exactly the factor that add excitement and that push the music forward.

What would happen if the strings just decided not to play those passages? The entire work would suffer. The drama and the beauty of this symphony would be lost.

It is the same in the theater. I once had an actor miss several rehearsals without being excused. When I confronted him about why he was not there, he said, "It doesn't really matter. I only have one line anyway, and I've already memorized it." I was furious. How could he believe that his role was so irrelevant that he could just make up his own time schedule?!

I explained to him that this was not about his "one line." We needed him on the stage reacting to the other actors and letting the other actors react to him. In the theater every role matters, and every role should be treated at if it were the main character. I explained that in the theater there are no small roles, only small actors. And I asked him if he wanted to be a small actor or step up and do his job.

This situation often occurs in teams. Team members do not see their role and their responsibilities as important toward the achievement of the team's goals. This often results in these team members not really stepping up and doing their jobs. It seems as though they are letting other team members do their jobs for them, simply because they don't see themselves as invested in the team. As a result, they become even less invested in the team and in the results that the team is working toward.

It is, therefore, important to be sure that every member of the team be able to articulate the team's desired outcome and that they understand how important their role is in achieving this outcome. It is important that each team member be invested in this

We want you to create a win-win-win situation, and this begins with understanding what each of these "wins" are. The first "win" is *your* desired outcome — both the obvious primary and less obvious secondary outcome — which we discussed in Chapter 7. The second "win" is the desired outcome of the other person, and the last "win" is accomplishing your common desired outcome while you serve the purpose of your organization, while you serve your "music."

outcome, and that they understand that without them — as without the strings in Dvorak's 9th — the results of the team's work will not be the quality that it needs to be in order to succeed.

_____

_____

_____

One last tough, but very important question: Could it be possible, in any way, that you, through your feelings about the other person, are keeping the team from accomplishing its goal in any way? If so, how? What do you need to be able to let go of this and help the team succeed? Please write this down and, if possible, find someone who can help you let go of whatever is standing in your way.

_____

_____

_____

Once you have an overview of your team's desired outcome and everyone is on board, set up a timeline for your project and create a transparent schedule of the steps necessary to accomplish this goal. Also, establish who is responsible for each of these steps. As you go through and create this schedule with your team, ask yourselves at every step, "Does this step serve our goal? Does this step serve our purpose?" If the answer to both of these questions is no, then this step should not be included in your schedule. It is important to respect everyone's time and talents. Something that does not serve your goal or your purpose is a waste of your time.

_____

_____

_____

We want you to create a win-win-win situation, and this begins with understanding what each of these "wins" are. The first "win" is *your* desired outcome — both the obvious primary and less obvious secondary outcome — which we discussed in chapter 7. The second "win" is the desired outcome of the other person, and the last "win" is accomplishing your common desired outcome while you serve the purpose of your organization, while you serve your "music."

Take a moment here to write down these outcomes, so that they remain very present in your conscious mind. As you do so, visualize accomplishing these outcomes, and visualize how wonderful you will feel when you succeed.

Your "Music"

_____

Your desired outcome	Our desired outcome	Their desired outcome

D

I

V

A   **ASSOCIATING WITH YOUR DIVA**

Chapter 19

Stop, Look, and Listen!
Connecting and Associating with Your Diva

In the last section we learned about what makes your diva tick, and we have established your desired outcome, their desired outcome and the common desired outcomes and purpose which you share. Now it is time to apply this information to your real-life interactions with your diva. It is time to bring together everything that you have learned and begin connecting and associating with your diva in a renewed, deeper, and more meaningful way.

The word "associate" is rooted in the latin word *associare* which means to "connect" to or "join with." In medieval English the word "associate" meant "to join together with a common purpose."

> The word "associate" is rooted in the latin word *associare* which means to "connect" to or "join with." In medieval English the word "associate" meant "to join together with a common purpose."

Even though you now understand your diva better than before and you have found your win-win-win situation, actually associating with and coming in contact with this person may still be difficult, and despite your best efforts, it may still cause misunderstandings or conflicts.

These misunderstandings and conflicts often occur simply because the two parties involved don't know how to communicate with each other. It's almost as though they speak different languages or live in two different worlds. Both sides can have the best of intentions, but for some reason, they fail to communicate. They fail to connect or join together, to associate with each other.

In this section we will focus on the factors that cause people to immediately connect with other and those that drive people apart, and I will show you how you can easily create bonds with others, so that each encounter you have is far more productive and engaging.

ESTABLISHING A COMMON GROUND

The well-known German trainer Vera Birkenbihl described communication as functioning in the following way:

Each of us is an island unto itself, and this island is made up of our experiences, beliefs, values, hobbies, interests, etc.

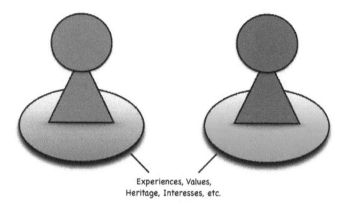

Experiences, Values,
Heritage, Interests, etc.

In a communication where two people have commonalities, both people involved in the conversation describe the other person as being interesting, intelligent, competent, and an all-round nice person. They find meetings productive and friendly, and they feel the other person understands them. They would like to see the other person again.

In a communication where two people don't have any commonalities, both parties describe the other person as being unfriendly, incompetent, unintelligent, and all-round boring. The meetings are not productive and they don't wish to associate with the person.

In picture C the two islands overlap. This means that the two people involved have some common ground, be it hobbies, interests, experiences, etc. The two people involved in this situation describe the other person as being interesting, intelligent, competent, and an all-round nice person. They find meetings productive and friendly, and feel the other person understands them. They would like to see the other person again.

Research has shown that if we manage — as in this example — to find some common ground with the other person, we will have a much greater chance of relating to them, and they will be able to relate to us.

THE THREE LEVELS TO CONNECT WITH YOUR DIVA

The three levels on which you can connect with your diva are the auditory level, the physical level, and on the level of common experiences and values. The third of these levels is the deepest. It is a basic human need to want to connect with other people. It gives us a sense of belonging. Finding similarities through common experiences, a common heritage, or through common values is the strongest of all connections. It gives us a pre-existing history with other person. This story of a dear friend of mine illustrates how you can begin to connect with others at the level of common experiences and values.

The three levels on which you can connect with your diva are the auditory level, the physical level, and on the level of common experiences and values.

BETTER THAN ANY MEDICINE

Karl is a physician and a good friend of our family. He has an excellent reputation and his patients love him. One day, he and I were talking about the many house calls he does and why his patients like him so much. The answer is simple. When he goes into the patients' homes — if he doesn't know the patients from previous visits — he spends at least part of his visit getting to know them, not just treating their symptoms.

When I asked him how he does this, he said, "In different ways. Often I look around to see what interests the person, then I ask them about it."

At Christmastime, he asks them about their Christmas tree, saying something like, "That's a beautiful tree! We haven't gotten ours yet — where did you find yours?" Or if he has already gotten his, he says something like, "That's a beautiful tree! We just got ours last week, but haven't had a chance to decorate it yet." He always speaks about things that genuinely interest him and connect him personally to the patient.

These conversations enable him to get to know the patient better and to observe how the patient is truly doing. Even if the amount of time that he spends with the patient is limited because of other house calls, he always tries to find at least one thing in common.

Karl does this instinctively, and his patients love him for it. He swears that this little step is the reason that his patients often get well so quickly. He says the most important part of the healing process is being seen and being taken seriously as a person and as a patient.

I mentioned mirroring to him, and he said it makes sense. We all want to connect with others at some level, especially if that person is important to us. For Karl, it is easiest to find something in common

> When you connect with others through finding common experiences or interests, these commonalities must be genuine and true. The other person will notice if you are not sincere, honest, and authentic.

with his patients to help them heal, especially when he is being invited into their most private sanctuary, their homes.

When connecting to others at the level of common experience and values, it is essential to remain sincere. Karl is there to care for his patients, and his interest in his patients is sincere. If, however, he had other motivations, such as to manipulate them, they would sense it and would not trust him.

A classic example of this happened to me not long ago. A telephone sales person called to sell me something. One of his first sentences was, "Laura. My sister's name is Laura!" Now, this may or may not be true. I don't know. All I can say is that I did not believe him. He was trying to create what was for me an unnatural bond for this situation, and in doing so, I resolved at that moment to hang up. Again, any attempt to find a connection — at any level — must be real and sincere.

One of the most interesting examples of connecting with people at the common experience level is the so-called Benjamin Franklin effect. In his autobiography Franklin refers to what he considers an old maxim.

"He that has once done you a kindness will be more ready to do you another, than he whom you yourself have obliged." He goes on to explain how his relationship to one of his rival legislators changed into a friendship.

"Having heard that he had in his library a certain very scarce and curious book, I wrote a note to him, expressing my desire of perusing that book, and requesting he would do me the favour of lending it to me for a few days. He sent it immediately, and I return'd it in about a week with another note, expressing strongly my sense of the favour. When we next met in the House, he spoke to me (which he had never done before), and with great civility; and he ever after manifested a readiness to serve me on all occasions, so that we became great friends, and our friendship continued to his death."

If you are still doubting the importance of being able to connect with others, consider Martin's story.

Recently, I was having lunch with a client of mine, Martin, who is on the board of a large nonprofit organization, and he confided in me that he was going to have to fire the executive director of the organization.

Martin, himself, is a high level executive for a large Fortune 500 company and has no problem with having to make difficult personnel decisions. In this case, however, he was somewhat reluctant. When I asked him why, he explained that he is new to the board and didn't want to come in and immediately make waves by firing the executive director. She had been on the job for not quite two years, and her numbers were way off. The organization would probably not be able to make payroll within six months.

We discuss different possibilities, how he might get by without firing her, but he sees no other solution. She clearly is not getting new funding to pay for the programs, and she seems to have little potential for improving. She seems willing to cooperate, but he genuinely does not believe that she is trainable. I ask him what he bases that on, and he tells me this example which he describes as the straw that broke the camel's back.

In order to help her raise funds, Martin arranges for the executive director to join him for lunch with a potential donor. This donor has already signaled he might be willing to donate a rather large sum to the organization, which could cover several more months of operating expenses.

I ask how it went, and Martin replies, "It was a disaster!"

He then continues, "Laura, you know as much about behavioral psychology and mirroring as I do. Picture this: You go to lunch with this important client and with a member of the board. It is obvious that the client is very physically active and mindful of his health. The client and the member of the board order small salads with chicken. What would you order?"

All I could do was laugh and ask, "Okay, so she ordered the fried onion-ring loaf with a mega-burger, huh?"

He answers, "Basically, yes with a couple of extra courses to add."

Through putting her personal desires above getting to know the potential donor, the director lost a donation that may have saved her organization. Was she wrong to eat a mega-burger and fried onion loaf? No. Was she wrong to eat a mega-burger and fried onion loaf at this particular meeting? Yes. This is not about doing what gives you pleasure. This is about connecting.

You can always eat the mega-burger and fried onion loaf another time, but you don't often get a second chance to make that proverbial first impression and to connect with the other person. The goal of this meeting was not the food, it was connecting, and this executive director failed to connect.

After the meeting, the donor told Martin that, given her sense of judgement at this particular meeting, he did not feel like he could trust her to competently manage the funds. Martin said he had to

> When you encounter another person, STOP: Pause and take a break from yourself and your own expectations. LOOK: Observe what the other person is doing, how they look, how they are dressed — literally SEE the other person. And LISTEN: Listen to what they say and how they say it.

agree with him. The sad thing is that she was not even aware of what she had done wrong.

In one fell swoop she had alienated a potential donor and a member of the board, both of whom considered healthy eating to be an important value in their lives. Had she ordered a salad or some other healthy dish, she would have communicated that health was something that she valued, too. In addition, she would have communicated that their time was valuable to her as well, because the menu item she ordered (apparently with several courses) took considerably longer to eat than the salads that they ordered.

For Martin it was clear she did not understand this basic element of human communication. He felt like she could not possibly improve on the poor results she had been getting.

Finding common ground in the values or interests of others can help not only in improving new or established relationships, it can also help in restoring estranged relationships.

The most effective way to find these commonalities is to ask questions and to show interest in the other person. If you are not able — or do not want — to immediately find a connection at the common experiences and values level, begin a little more simply with my *Stop Look and Listen!* rule.

STOP, LOOK, AND LISTEN!

When we teach children how to cross a street, we teach them to Stop, Look, and Listen! They should always stop before entering the street, look both ways, and listen to hear if any cars may be approaching. Only when they are absolutely sure it is safe to cross the street, should they proceed.

The same rule holds true when you are building relationships. When you encounter another person, STOP: Pause and take a break from yourself and your own expectations. LOOK: Observe what the other person is doing, how they look, how they are dressed — literally SEE the other person. And LISTEN: Listen to what they say and how they say it.

In the next three chapters we will further discuss how to connect with the other person at the visual and auditory levels.

Before we go on, take a moment to reflect on your relationship to your diva. What common experiences might you have? What common values do you have? Have you been to or lived in the same places? Do you have any colleagues or acquaintances in common?

_____

_____

_____

_____

_____

_____

_____

_____

Chapter 20

Stop, Look and Listen!
Tools to Connect with Your Diva

STOP, LOOK, AND LISTEN! HOW TO BEGIN

STOP!

The first step is to STOP, to pause and allow yourself to be in the moment. Allow yourself to be fully present with the other person. Neutral, present, and open.

When we encounter another person, especially when we encounter our diva, most of us tend to already be thinking about what we want to say and how we want to appear to this person. We begin to form answers to questions that they haven't yet asked. We want to sell ourselves as being in control.

The challenge with this tendency is that it is almost impossible to get to know or understand the other person if we are concentrating on ourselves.

So, STOP! Take a moment to allow yourself to become centered, focused, and mindful of the other person. Let go of any possible expectations you may have of the conversation, and allow yourself to be fully aware and observant of the other person.

LOOK!

Connecting to another person at the visual level requires sharpening your visual skills. Observe their body language, facial expressions, even their breathing. As you observe them, mirror their body language and breathing. It allows you to connect with them and, literally, feel where they are emotionally.

WARNING:

One of the most common skills taught in sales and communication seminars is mirroring. Students are taught to mirror to establish rapport with the customer and then to use this established relationship to manipulate the customer into buying something.

Mirroring is a powerful tool, but if you are not sincere and respectful with your intentions, the other person will sense it and not trust you. The only reason, in my opinion, to use mirroring is to sincerely get to know the other person better.

Mirroring is a powerful tool, but, just as the sales person who told me that his sister's name is Laura, if you are not sincere and respectful with your intentions, the other person will sense it and not trust you. The only reason, in my opinion, to use mirroring is to sincerely get to know the other person better.

ONE VALUABLE USE OF MIRRORING IN MY WORK

One of the most difficult musical instruments to teach is the voice. This is because we can't see the instrument.

Just last week one of my students said, "You always know exactly what I'm doing wrong! How do you do that?"

Well, what I do is I calibrate, or mirror, the state of my students. I match their physiology and their breath, and, in this state, I literally feel in my body where their tensions are. I feel what they are doing wrong, and I correct it. Most good teachers and doctors do this instinctively. They are not consciously aware of the process, they just want to help their student or patient. This process is known as **pacing or calibrating**.

HOW THE PROCESS WORKS

To practice this process, find a partner — someone you trust — to do this exercise with you.

STEP 1. ESTABLISH RAPPORT – CALIBRATING OR PACING

- Put yourself in a neutral or positive emotional state.
- Observe the posture, body language, facial expressions, and breath of the other person.
- Mirror their physiology, allowing yourself to step into their state of being. Make sure that you also match the rhythm of their breath. You will find that the more you are connected to them, the easier and more natural this process is.
- Observe how your body responds to the mirroring to better understand the other person.

STEP 2. LEAD

If you want to help the other person change their physical or mental state, slowly change your physiology from the mirrored state into the desired state. For the purpose of this exercise, slowly change your physiology and observe how the other person begins to follow you.

For example, when I am teaching, I mirror my students to understand where unnecessary tensions are. As I correct their vocal technique, I bring my body into the desired state. If I have connected well with them, they will automatically mirror me into the desired state.

If I have not successfully connected with them (this occurs most often when they are fearful or overly self-involved), I begin the process again until we are closely connected.

In a conflict situation, you can use pacing and leading to help the other person calm down. By matching their physiology and tone of voice, you signal subconsciously that you see and hear them. Once rapport is established, begin to slow down and lead them to the desired state by slowly going into the desired state yourself.

EXERCISE:

Find a partner, and ask them to tell you about their last vacation. As they are doing this, match their physiology and tone of voice as naturally and unaffected as possible. Mirror their posture. Mirror their breathing. Mirror the speed at which they are speaking.

What do you observe? What did you find easy to do? What was more difficult? How did your partner experience the exercise?

_____

_____

_____

Now change the situation. Ask your partner to tell you about a conflict situation they have experienced. Again, mirror their behavior.

What do you observe? What did you find easy to do? What was more difficult? How did your partner experience the exercise? What was different from before (the vacation)?

_____

_____

_____

After you have completed mirroring the conflict situation exercise, ask your partner to tell you about the conflict situation again. This time, however, do not mirror your partner. Try as best you can to do the opposite. For example, if they lean forward, you should lean

You already have the skills you need to interpret body language.

back. If they speak loudly and quickly, you should speak slowly and quietly.

How does this situation differ from the situation where you mirrored your partner? Is it easier or more difficult to counter them? What does your partner observe?

_____

_____

_____

After you have completed the repeated conflict situation, ask your partner to tell you about the conflict situation a third time, but this time be even more upset and emotional about the situation. Mirror their behavior (body language and tone of voice), and then after you feel in sync with them, begin to relax your pace, to lead them to become calmer. Did it work? did they also slow down? Did they begin to follow you? If not, try it again. Keep experimenting until you figure out how long you need to calibrate their behavior before you can begin to lead.

_____

_____

_____

WHEN TO USE MIRRORING

Use mirroring and pacing and leading anytime you want to better understand and connect with another person. Practicing this skill will help you become much more sensitive to the inner state of the other person, and therefore it will help you understand his or her needs.

DON'T FALL INTO THIS TRAP!

Body language gurus often like to sell the idea that, if only you understand what the gestures mean, you can interpret the bodily signals of the person you are talking to. They assert you can basically read people's minds. This is simply not true. Defining gestures out of context is an oversimplification of the complex nature of nonverbal communication.

You already have the skills you need to interpret body language. For example, have you ever met someone you know well and noticed that something is wrong? You may have even been able to "read their minds"? In these cases you use your skills of observation and comparison.

Because you know the person well, you know their body language and how they act in everyday situations. You recognize how the voice and body signals change. This ability to observe and compare is what counts in interpreting body language. You notice the differences, observe further signals, verbal and nonverbal, and are able to understand what this person is thinking or feeling.

Furthermore, because this person is important to you, you observe this person more closely. In doing so, you naturally mirror them, you calibrate their behavior. As soon as you do this, you empathize with them. The only difference between you and the "experts" is practice. They are able to calibrate and mirror more quickly and observe any changes in behavioral patterns. From this and through strategic questions, they surmise reasons for changes in behavior.

LISTEN!

In his book *Yes! 50 Secrets from the Science of Persuasion* Cialdini, Goldstein, and Martin site a study on mirroring done with waiters and waitresses. The researchers wanted to see if mirroring the customer had a direct effect on the amount of tips waiters and waitresses received. The results were astounding.

The servers were divided into two groups. The first group simply wrote down the orders of their customers without repeating what the customer said. For example, the customer would say, "I would like the baked salmon with rice," and the server would be simply nod or say, "Okay, thank you" but would not repeat the order.

In the second group the server would repeat the order while writing it down and would match the inflection and exact word choice that the customer used — in a natural way.

The results were amazing. In comparison to the first group where the servers did not repeat the order, the second group had an increase of in tips of up to 70%. But why does this happen?

WE WANT TO BE UNDERSTOOD

There are two reasons why mirroring works. First, we want to feel like we are understood. Looking at the research from the restaurant example, we can often relate to the customer whose waiter does not repeat his order back. The waiter may smile back at us and say thank

Mirroring works because we want to find ourselves in the other person.

you, but until the order comes, we are never absolutely certain that we were understood.

This level of insecurity increases greatly if the waiter doesn't even write the order down. We're amazed when the waiter gets the order right, but the unsure feeling we had while waiting for the order to arrive is commonly reflected in the amount of tip we give.

When we mirror others, it not only helps us to better understand and relate to them, it helps them feel as if they are understood and taken seriously. They are then more willing to trust us and, as in the Birkenbihl description, they subconsciously will find us more interesting, intelligent, and competent. They will consider the relationship as meaningful and worthwhile.

WE WANT TO FIND OURSELVES IN THE OTHER PERSON

The second reason mirroring works is that we want to find ourselves in the other person. We are by nature somewhat narcissistic. We like looking at ourselves and listening to ourselves. If you put one or two large mirrors in a room with people, you will find them sneaking looks at themselves. Perhaps to make sure that their hair or makeup is still in place, but more often than not, it's just simply to look at themselves, even while talking to other people. This is even true of people who say they don't like themselves, and can't stand to look at themselves in the mirror!

Humans like to find themselves reflected in the environment around them, be it in mirrors or monuments or gravestones or selfies. Mirroring is one way to help others find themselves in us. It gives them a higher sense of self-worth, and this in turn immediately builds more trust and understanding.

CONNECTING AT THE AUDITORY LEVEL – INFLECTION

At the auditory level there are two ways of connecting to the other person: the inflection of speech, and the content of the spoken text. In the following chapters we will concentrate on recognizing the content and intention of what is being said. Here I would like to focus on the inflection.

Have you ever called a service center to report a problem with, let's say, your phone service, and experienced something like this:

You: (angry, upset) I just got my phone bill from last month, and I am furious!! It is completely wrong!! I don't even know half of the numbers on this bill, and there is no way that I am paying this!!

Call Center Representative: (very calm, speaking slowly) Now, I can understand that you are upset, but let's calm down. I'm sure that….

You: (even angrier) Upset? I am not upset, I'm furious. You calm down; I want this problem solved NOW!

The call center service person doesn't seem to understand you at all, and quite frankly, it seems as if he is condescending. You don't trust this person to be of help in any capacity.

This is an example of a lack of mirroring. Mirroring doesn't only occur at the visual level, it occurs at the auditory level as well. And because emotion is primarily communicated through inflection or tone of voice, establishing common ground at the auditory level is crucial.

Had the call center employee met your inflection — the speed and dynamic at which you were speaking, you would have felt as if you were being heard. The conversation would gone more like this:

You: (angry, upset) I just got my phone bill from last month, and I am furious!! It is completely wrong!! I don't even know half of the numbers on this bill, and there is no way that I am paying this!!

Call Center Representative: (upset, amazed — matching the tone of voice you used) Wait a minute. You don't know half of the numbers on this bill? I can certainly understand why you do not want to pay this! Wait a minute. Let me get your information so that I can look at this bill. (Beginning to slow down and lead the conversation) Please give me your name again. . .

This time the customer felt understood.

With auditory pacing there are three main aspects to observe: the inflection of the other person's voice, the content of the what the other person is saying, and last but not least, the intent of the other person. Here we will begin with mirroring the inflection.

INFLECTION MIRRORING EXERCISE

The inflection of the voice has to do with the sound, speed, pitch, and intensity of the voice. We associate the inflection of the voice with the emotion the person seems to be feeling or emoting.

In order to consciously mirror the inflection of the voice, find a partner and do the following exercise. Again, as with physically mirroring another person, it is important that your motivation is sincere, not manipulative.

- Put yourself in a neutral or positive emotional state.

- Observe the inflection of the voice, the speed at which the other person is speaking, how loudly or softly, the intensity of the voice and the breathing. What emotions do you hear in the voice?
- As naturally as possible, use your voice to mirror their vocal inflection, allowing yourself to really step into their state of being. If you are truly connected to them, this will happen automatically at a subconscious level.
- Observe how your body responds to the mirroring to better understand the other person.
- If you wish to change the emotional state of the other person, slowly begin to change your emotional state after you are certain that rapport has been established.

What are your observations? What did you find easy to do and what was more difficult? How did your partner experience the exercise? Did you seem natural or affected?

_____

_____

_____

_____

_____

_____

_____

_____

_____

_____

Chapter 21

Stop, Look, and Listen!
What the Diva Says Matters

Now that you have practiced mirroring the physiology and inflection of your partner, it is time to observe the content of what your partner is saying, so that you can learn to mirror it as well.

WHAT THEY SAY MATTERS

When you are establishing rapport with another person, what *they* say matters. It is important to notice exactly verbatim what they are saying. Which vocabulary are they using? How are they describing what they want or need?

In mirroring content there are three aspects to watch out for: 1) the specific vocabulary, including the grammatical structure, that they use, 2) the predominant sensory language that they use, and 3) the assumption that the content of their story is real.

SPECIFIC VOCABULARY AND GRAMMATICAL STRUCTURE

One of the most common mistakes we tend to make in communication is to assume we know what the other person is trying to communicate, and this begins at the most basic level of communication, the choice of vocabulary.

When you mirror someone at the auditory level, observe and mirror their choice of vocabulary. This is especially important to ensure you are not adding your interpretation of their content to the conversation.

In our service center example above, the caller said he was "angry," but the customer service person said he could understand the caller was "upset." Depending on the interpretation of both parties, tension could escalate substantially. If the caller were of the opinion that being "upset" is the same as being "angry," then everything is fine. If, however, the customer is of the opinion that "upset" is very different from being "angry," the service representative would have a problem on his hands. It is always best to mirror the exact word back

> When you are establishing rapport with another person, what *they* say matters.

We often subconsciously impose our definition of a word or phrase on another person in that we presume to understand what they mean by choosing this word or phrase. We then, in turn, choose our own words to mirror back what we think they are saying. This can be very misleading and can easily lead to miscommunications.

and, as in the case of generalizations, it is best to ask the person what he means by the word he or she just used.

GENERALIZATIONS

We often subconsciously impose our definition of a word or phrase on another person in that we presume to understand what they mean by choosing this word or phrase. We then, in turn, choose our own words to mirror back what we think they are saying. This can be very misleading and can easily lead to miscommunications.

A generalization is a word that has a broad meaning which, although we think we know what it means, it is actually impossible to understand without asking for further information.

One example is the word "stress." Although we think we know what the word means, it is impossible to know what "stress" means to another person without asking them.

A typical example of this misunderstanding happened to me when my children were very small. A well-meaning friend saw that I seemed a bit stressed-out and asked if I had a lot of stress.

I answered, "Yes, things were really difficult."

He then said, "I know, you work so hard. Don't you think you could cut back on your work hours while the children are still young?"

I almost flipped out! You see, for me work was pure relaxation. I love my work and couldn't get enough of it. For me, stress was putting my children to bed. I loved playing with them, I loved doing crafts with them and being with them, but the almost hour-long ritual of bringing them to bed was driving me crazy.

A colleague of mine voiced my opinion well: Better to sing ten operas than to put one child into bed! And yet, this well-meaning friend assumed that I was so exhausted and tense because I was "working" too much outside of the home. For me, it was because I was "working" too little.

Other good examples of a generalization would be the words "love" or "friendship" or "happiness." Who can truly say what "love," "friendship," or "happiness" means to another person?

When we are mirroring the context of what someone is saying and we notice that they use a generalization, it is important to ask them what they mean by that word. For example, to ask, "How and when do you experience this?" Then use the vocabulary that they use to describe the word in your conversation.

GRAMMATICAL STRUCTURE

As with vocabulary and sensory language, another aspect of the spoken language to observe and mirror is the grammatical structures the other person is using. If, for example, the other person is speaking in passive voice, then match their use of the passive voice. If, for some reason, they speak in the past or future tense, mirror it. It will help you to understand them better, and they will feel much more connected to you.

SENSORY LANGUAGE

In mirroring what others say, it is important to observe the sensory language or sensory canal that the other person uses.

All of us think in pictures, sounds, and feelings. Our thoughts are merely interpretations by our sensory organs of what we see, hear, feel, smell and taste. In addition, the learning process and thought process is aided and filtered by our senses.

For example, some people are visual learners. They best learn information after they have seen it. Others learn best by hearing the information. Still others learn fastest if they can physically move around while learning. Most of us learn through a combination of these.

In order to understand how the other person is thinking and processing information, it is helpful to recognize the sensory language that they are speaking. Again, our goal is to better understand the other person and to find a common ground.

EXAMPLES OF SENSORY LANGUAGE:

Typical phrases used by a visual learner include; *it looks like, let's see, look at how this is, look at this idea, looks like a good idea to me, the way I see it is.*

Typical phrases used by an auditory learner include: *it sounds like, sounds like a good idea to me, listen to this idea, I'd say that, etc.*

Typical phrases used by a kinesthetic learner are *just do it, just try it out, this feels right to me, let's feel this idea out, how does that feel to you?*

SENSORY LANGUAGE: WHO DO YOU THINK WOULD MAKE THE SALE?

Paul wants to buy a new stereo. He has just moved into a new apartment and his old stereo is too big and clunky for his living room. On Saturday morning, Paul goes into Stereo Store A and is greeted by John in the showroom.

Another cause for miscommunication I have often observed is disbelief. The listener mentally discredits the story or changes the story to something more plausible. As soon as we begin to do this, we begin to separate ourselves from the other person and their experience.

John: "How are you today? How can I help you?"

Paul: "I'm looking for a new stereo. One that takes up less space. I'd like it to be black and sleek with lots of lights."

John: "Well, this model here has an incredible sound. You can hear how strong the bass is, and with this equalizer you can adjust the sound to be absolutely perfect for the acoustics of the room."

They look at a couple more stereos. Paul thanks John for his time, and he leaves. He then goes into Stereo Store B to see what stereos they have and is greeted by Trudy.

Paul: "I'm looking for a new stereo. One that takes up less space. I'd like it to be black and sleek with lots of lights."

Trudy: "When you say, 'Takes up less space,' how small would you like the stereo to be? How should it look?"

Paul: "Well, it would basically be under the television, so it needs to fit into a space about this size." He shows Trudy the size with his hands.

Trudy: "Okay. Let's see what we have. In that size we have two models, both of which have excellent reputations, but neither comes in black. The dark silver one has a lot of lights. Could that fit what you're looking for?"

In both examples Paul states that he is thinking about the visual aspects of the stereo, and he clearly uses visual language. In trying to help Paul, John talks about the sound of the stereo and uses predominantly auditory language.

Trudy, on the other hand, mirrors Paul's visual language and asks clarifying questions in order to understand what Paul is looking for. Although we haven't followed these conversations to the conclusion of the sale, it is clear that Trudy has a much better chance of finding what Paul needs than John does.

BELIEVING WHAT SEEMS TO YOU TO BE UNBELIEVABLE

Another cause for miscommunication I have often observed is disbelief. The listener for whatever reason cannot believe the content of what they're being told. They immediately mentally discredit or change the story to something more plausible. As soon as we begin to do this, we begin to separate ourselves from the other person and their experience.

It is well and good to make a mental note to yourself that this story is, for you, improbable, but the "I'll believe it when I see it" attitude can greatly hinder communication and your ability to create common ground.

This is best demonstrated by a conversation I had some time back with a dear friend of mine.

Harry is a very good, sought-after psychiatrist. One day, as I was visiting him at his home, we were discussing different case studies he was working on. One such case was a woman who genuinely believed that she had been abducted by extra-terrestrial beings and had been taken not only into their UFO but also to their planet.

I found this case particularly interesting, and so I asked him how he handles such a case. Does he put himself into the reality of the patient, allowing himself to suspend "reality" and believe that she was abducted, or does he remain "rational" and communicate that her experience cannot be "real." He gave the question back to me and asked me how I would treat the patient.

In my work on communication, the goal is to better understand the other person and to be able to better communicate with him or her than to be "right." In the world of psychiatry, the goal is to heal the person. There is an assumption of a healthy psyche. Yet, the initial phases of psychiatry should be, in my opinion, to better understand the person — the same goal as in communication.

My answer was that I would, for the sake of better understanding the person, believe her story. I would believe she had been abducted, and in the course of asking her many questions about the abduction (just imagine if it were true!) I would mirror her breathing, and observe when and where she was tense. It would give me the chance to get to know her better — what her experiences were, what her fears were, perhaps even what led to this suspended reality.

He found that interesting and said that is, at least initially, what he has to do in order to understand her reality.

Most commonly people don't tell us of extra-terrestrial experiences. Most commonly the stories we hear have to do with experiences in our everyday lives.

A wonderful example of this type of miscommunication happened to Bob, the CEO of a small IT company. Bob was interviewing prospective employees for a new programming position in his company, and, after the first round of interviews, he asked his first choice, Samantha, to come to the company for an orientation meeting. At this meeting Samantha was to find out what this position entailed and both Bob and Samantha were to then decide if her employment was a good fit.

It so happened that I knew both Bob and Samantha personally, and what then happened was fascinating. Bob was not sure of the

> In my work on communication, the goal is to better understand the other person and to be able to better communicate with him or her than to be "right."

date the two of them agreed upon for the meeting, and so he called and left a message on Samantha's voicemail asking her to please call him back on his cell phone. He did not mention in the message that the office would be closed for the next week.

She tried this number several times and got no answer. She then called the office number and heard the message that the office would be closed for the next week (during that week, she was supposed to meet with Bob). She left a message on the office answering machine stating that she assumed the meeting was cancelled, since the office is closed, and would he please contact her for a new date.

Bob's Reality: Samantha did not follow his orders and call him back on his cell phone. She instead called the office and cancelled the appointment. He didn't get this message until over a week later. He was furious.

Samantha's Reality: Bob didn't answer her multiple phone calls to his cell phone and therefore wasted her time. She was still open to working for him but was much more hesitant than before. She, too, was angry and frustrated.

When Bob finally called Samantha back, she told him that she tried to call his cell phone many times, but no one answered it. Because there were no calls on his cell phone from her, he didn't believe her.

To him, she was unreliable and was lying to him. He didn't hire her, and he wasn't interested in understanding what went wrong in the communication. He actually missed out on hiring for his company one of the best programmers in the field, and ended up hiring someone who was neither qualified nor reliable. Samantha took a position at a much larger IT company.

In hearing about this wonderful example of miscommunication, I asked Samantha what happened. When she told me she had tried calling, but Bob didn't answer his cell phone and there was no voicemail to leave a message, I asked to see the number that she dialed.

Apparently, the connection from Bob's phone was poor when he left the message on her voicemail, and she misheard the number by one digit. So, Bob's presumption that Samantha lied was wrong. He missed out on having an excellent employee just because he couldn't entertain the fact that her reality was different from his.

When you are mirroring someone and you find yourself in a state of disbelief, allow yourself to come back to the reality of the other person. If you don't, you will be carrying on two separate and distinctly different dialogues in your head, and it will not be possible to observe and connect with the other person.

Allow yourself to suspend your own reality and set yourself in the situation being described. More often than not, what they are explaining truly did happen — however implausible it may seem — and most often, you will get to know them much more deeply than you imagined possible.

EXERCISE:

Over the next days and weeks, each time you find yourself conversing with another person, consciously mirror their content. Use their vocabulary, their sensory language, and their grammatical structure.

What do you observe?

_____

_____

_____

_____

_____

_____

_____

_____

Chapter 22

Stop, Look, and Listen!
The Diva's Intent and Your Interpretation

INTENT AND INTERPRETATION

Yet another communication trap that often occurs is when the listener believes he understands what the speaker is trying or intending to say. We always interpret what is being said through our own filters of experience and emotion, and these filters often cause us to interpret information very differently than the other person intended.

Therefore, another very important element to observe while establishing common ground at the auditory level is intent vs. interpretation. This ability will help you recognize the intention of what is being said by the other person and how you are interpreting what you hear.

The following two models will help you become more aware of intent and interpretation. The first is Friedemann Schulz von Thun's *Communication Square*, which shows how the intentions of the speaker can be very different than those of the listener. The second is a communication and change management model, which was initially created by Gregory Bateson and later expanded upon by Robert Dilts, called *The Logical Levels*.

> Yet another communication trap that often occurs is when the listener believes he understands what the speaker is trying or intending to say. We always interpret what is being said through our own filters of experience and emotion, and these filters often cause us to interpret information very differently than the other person intended.

FOUR-SIDES MODEL

Friedemann Schulz von Thun, a German psychologist and communications researcher, argued that in communication both the speaker and the listener have intent. In other words, any given sentence that we say has an intention, and when this intention is interpreted differently by the speaker than by the listener, miscommunications will occur.

For example, if I were to tell my husband that he has not taken out the garbage, he may interpret this sentence as simply being a fact — he has not yet taken out the garbage — or he may interpret this sentence as being a complaint or order from my side (what Schulz von Thun calls an "appeal") that he should take out the garbage right now!

Schulz von Thun argues that there are four types of intent on both the side of the speaker and of the listener, which he describes in his *Communication Square*: 1) Factual information, 2) Appeal, 3) Relationship, and 4) Self-revelation.

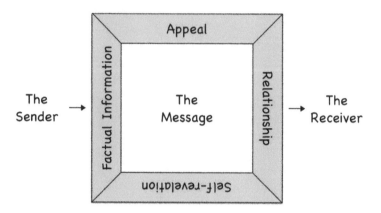

To better understand all four sides to the Communications Square, let's use the example from above where I, in this case the speaker, tell my husband, the listener, that he has not yet taken out the garbage.

FACTUAL SIDE

On the factual side the speaker simply wants to convey factual information. In other words, the garbage is still in the garbage can and has not yet been taken outside. Period. There is no hidden agenda, no other message or meaning other than the garbage is still in the house.

SELF-REVEALING SIDE

On the self-revealing side, the speaker reveals something about his or her own personality. Depending on inflection the sentence is said, *"You didn't take out the garbage"* could reveal many different things.

It could reveal that the speaker is worried about the garbage stinking and attracting rodents or bugs. It could reveal the speaker is concerned because for some reason they are not capable of taking the garbage out and don't know how it can otherwise be done. It could also reveal the speaker is not physically there to take out the garbage and, although they would greatly like to help the listener, they are not in a position to do so.

RELATIONSHIP SIDE

On the relationship side of the Four-Sides Model, the speaker expresses how the relationship between the speaker and the listener is and what they think of each other.

The sentence "*You didn't take out the garbage,*" could refer to an agreement made about taking the garbage out. It could imply anger about the agreement not being honored, or it could imply a question about how the other person values the relationship.

APPEAL SIDE

On the appeal side of the Four-Sides Model the speaker is giving the listener a command. The speaker is letting the listener know that there is something to be done, and the speaker expects the listener to do what is expected.

With our example of "*You didn't take out the garbage,*" the speaker is ordering (or appealing to) the listener to take the garbage out.

THE INTENTION (EXPECTATION) OF THE LISTENER

Just as the speaker has intention when he or she is saying something, the listener also has intention — or expectations. The listener interprets the message depending on which of the sides they believe the speaker is speaking from.

If the listener hears "You didn't take out the garbage," as coming from the factual side, he she will think, "True, I haven't taken out the garbage."

If he hears it as coming from the self-revealing side, he may think, "O dear, the speaker is worried about the garbage." Or, "The speaker thinks that I am lazy."

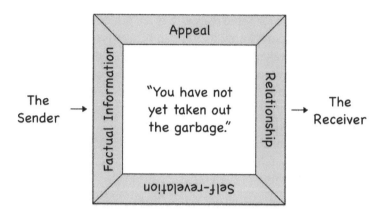

If he hears it as coming from the relationship side, he may think, "I need to take out the garbage to keep peace in the relationship."

Or if he hears it as being spoken from the appeal side, he may think, "The speaker is ordering me around! How dare she!"

So, for example, if the sender is sending with intent of factual information, but the receiver is hearing the message as in this last example, as an appeal, you can imagine how angry the receiver might be. Although the sender had neither the desire nor intention to anger the receiver, a miscommunication happened.

To put this situation in our diagram it would look like this:

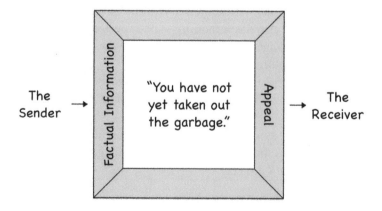

If you realize that the other person is hearing with a different intention than you, it may be helpful to share that observation with them. I write "may" be helpful, because when emotions are high, it is not always possible to reach the person simply be mentioning what you observe.

No matter what, observing differences in intention will help you better understand the person. This, in turn, will help you in reaching your — and their — goals.

EXERCISE:

In every conversation you lead in the next weeks, observe not only what your partner is saying but how he is saying it. Are their intentions always the same as yours?

_____

_____

_____

LOGICAL LEVELS

Another helpful model to aid a better understand someone's intention is Robert Dilts's *Logical Levels*.

The *Logical Levels* is an excellent communication and change management tool which helps us understand thought processes and how change affects structure. You will find more information about the history and usage of the Logical Levels in the endnotes. For our purposes here, this is an excellent tool to help you become more aware of the language that others use and to be able to both understand them and better communicate with them.

The *Logical Levels* is an excellent communication and change management tool which helps us understand thought processes and how change affects structure.

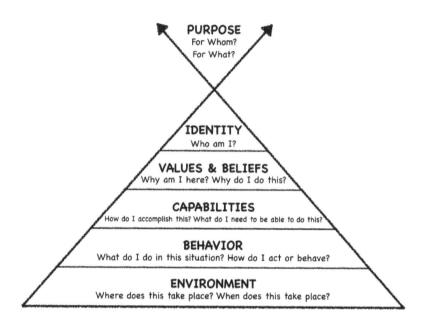

Each of us lives and thinks at different "levels" at different times, and each level automatically encompasses the levels underneath it. Research has shown that people who tend to focus on the three top levels (Values, Identity, and Purpose) tend to be much more successful and can handle change much more easily than people who predominantly focus on the three lower levels (Environment, Behavior, and Capabilities).

For example, let us take someone who has to give a talk. If this person focuses predominantly on the environment they will not be as flexible in different situations. "I can't give the talk here. The room is too big!" Or, "The podium is in the wrong place. I can't stand over there."

On the other hand, someone who is instead focused on their sense of purpose is willing to give their talk any and everywhere. It doesn't matter if they are on a street corner or in a small room or in a large auditorium, they are focused on the message that they want to share with their audience. They know who they are (Identity) and why they are there (Values and Purpose), and, as a result, they are much more flexible and less prone to being distracted by the details of the lower levels. (By the way, stage fright, by its nature, is at the lower three levels: Capabilities — I don't know if I have the skills I need for this or if I am good enough, Behavior — what if I do something wrong or make a mistake, and Environment — this room is too . . .)

We once had a secretary who was focused on the environment and behavior levels. Everyday I would walk past her desk on the way to my office and ask how she was. The answer was almost always, "It is too cold in here." Or, "There is too much dust in here." Or, "I can't believe how so-and-so acted today." Her focus was not on her purpose for being there.

Don't get me wrong, I liked her. We always got along well, but I was amazed at how distracted she was by her environment and how other people behaved. This distraction had a huge impact on her work — both on the quality of the work she did and on how people interacted with her. They often tried to avoid her.

The chairman of the department was at loss as to what to do. He changed how the furniture in the office was arranged. He increased the temperature of the room, but it was then too hot. It seemed that he could not create an environment in which she could be happy.

Eventually, she left us, and her replacement was the absolute opposite. If you asked her to type something for you, her answer was not that she had no time or that her fingers are too cold (literally an answer that we on occasion got from her predecessor). She would say, "Of course!" If she didn't think that she could get it done in the timeframe given, she would say something like, "Of course I can get this done, but not by then." Then she would say by when it would be done. If that wasn't soon enough, she would find a solution together with the other person. Her focus was on why she was there (her sense of purpose), and who she was — an excellent secretary (Identity) — who did her best to find excellent solutions for those working with her (Values).

Did they always find the perfect solution? No. But they came much closer to finding solutions than they did with her predecessor. The result was that everyone, faculty and staff, were much happier, much more creative, much more willing to work together, and much more focused on moving forward and accomplishing more than they had been before. The difference was amazing.

In your situation with your diva, the *Logical Levels* are an excellent way of observing how the other person communicates. If you notice that you tend to speak at one level, let's say the values level, and

Listen to what they say and which level they are speaking from. If they communicate with you at a different level, adjust your speech to match theirs. In other words, realize what they are saying and mirror this back to them, so that you can better understand what their needs are.

the other person speaks predominantly from the behavioral level, miscommunications may occur.

Listen to what they say and which level they are speaking from. If they communicate with you at a different level, adjust your speech to match theirs. In other words, realize what they are saying and mirror this back to them, so that you can better understand what their needs are.

If you notice that they consistently communicate at one of the lower levels, use the language of that level to create a common language and then allow yourself to appeal to their higher self.

For example with our first secretary, one thing that the chairman could have done was to say, "I know that the room is very cold today, and we'll try to get it changed. I find it amazing how you manage — even in this cold room — to help us make our department stronger. Thank you for being the excellent secretary that you are and for helping us accomplish our goals."

What happens in this exchange is that the chairman recognized and mirrored back the language of the environmental level, and then he appealed to her higher self, her sense of identity, her values, and her sense of purpose. He causes her to think about the other levels.

Would this have changed her immediately? No. This is not a one-time solution to unhappy employees. To bring real change, he would need to repeat this type of exchange in different ways and in different situations. Hopefully, through this she would then begin to focus on the higher levels on her own.

I am reminded of a personal story of when my daughter was doing an exchange year in the USA. She was having problems in her Latin class, and it looked like she might not do well. She knew that her grades from that exchange year would not count on her record here in Germany, and so she decided to slack off a bit. She happened to mention that to my mother, who lived nearby. She told my mother that it didn't really matter if studied or not, because it didn't count anyway. My mother, who had been a teacher and a guidance counselor for many, many years, just looked at her and said, "Stephanie, that is not right, and we do what is right! We always give our best."

She appealed to Stephanie's value system. Stephanie had been thinking predominantly at the behavioral level (what I do doesn't matter, therefore I can do whatever I want), and her grandmother quickly reminded her that those were not the values she should strive toward. Stephanie got to work and aced the class. We were very proud of her and grateful to my mother.

We often need to be reminded of who we are and what our values are, and often just in reflecting on these two things, everything that we need to do or learn falls into place and becomes very clear. Focusing on the higher levels — your values, identity, and sense of purpose — both for yourself and others will lead to success.

EXERCISE:

During the next several days, observe your conversations with other people. What do you talk about? At which level of the *Logical Levels* are you communicating?

_____

_____

_____

_____

At which level are the others communicating?

_____

_____

_____

_____

If you notice a difference between your level(s) and theirs, mirror them. Change your focus to match theirs. What happens?

_____

_____

_____

_____

If they are speaking at a level lower than yours, mirror that level and then appeal to their higher sense of self. What happens then?

_____

_____

_____

_____

Chapter 23

Let It Go!
When Divas Don't Cooperate

When I began working on this book, I told a dear friend of mine about it. She happens to be head of HR for a large international company here in Germany. She was interested in the project, and after a couple of minutes of discussing it, she laughed and said, "But what if the diva simply doesn't want to cooperate?"

At first I wanted to dismiss the question, but here was someone I highly respected who had worked with challenging personalities at all levels. Her point was not only valid but essential to consider. What if, through all of your best efforts, you are not able to reach any level of cooperation with your diva?

Undoubtedly, there will be situations in which a diva will simply not want to cooperate. These situations are much more seldom than one might think, but they do happen. What should you do then?

> There will be situations in which a diva will simply not want to cooperate. These situations are much more seldom than one might think, but they do happen.

A PERSONAL CASE STUDY

When I was between my studies at Ohio State and Duke University, I was hired to be the administrative assistant for the Classical Studies Department at Duke. The administrative assistant is responsible for the departmental budget, office personnel, scheduling, and running the day-to-day functions of the office and department.

After I accepted the job, I was told that my first task was to fire my secretary. Diana (not her real name) was from eastern Europe and could neither speak nor type English well. She could not understand people on the phone, and she typed at a pace of one word per minute. Yes, one word. She was charming, and I could only assume her charms and international flair caused her to get the job. She had been there a little over a year, and definitely thought that she was the boss in the situation.

I understood it was my responsibility to fire her, and I accepted this responsibility without hesitation. After about a week or so into my job, I began the process. I contacted Duke's personnel offices to inform them of the situation, and was met with an answer that surprised me. We were not, under any circumstances, allowed to fire her. The department had hired her against the recommendation of the personnel office. She was in the Duke system and could not be fired. Our only chance was to find her another job at Duke.

You can imagine the atmosphere in our shared office.

Diana, knowing full-well that she could not be fired, became more arrogant then ever. She reported me to personnel as being discriminatory against her as a foreigner, and her case was taken over by affirmative action. If you are familiar with discrimination cases, this was the kiss of death for my situation.

Starting at that moment, everything I did, said, or wrote was under scrutiny. In addition, I was doing two jobs: hers and mine. Because she was not capable of typing in English — when she did, there were so many mistakes that it had to be redone anyway — all of the faculty brought their letters to me to type. Because she was not capable of answering the phone, this, too fell on my shoulders. The only thing that she could do — although the faculty didn't trust her to do this either — was to use the copying machine. And we really didn't have that many copies to make.

Two things helped me through this situation. First, in a discussion with my older brother, who was himself an executive in a large corporation, he told me how I handled the situation could be one of the most important things I would ever do. He said I had the power to truly be of help both to the secretary and to the department. He stated that how I treat my secretary would either help her to grow and move on to a position of success or to fail. I could truly make a difference in her life. I could help this woman whom I really did not want to be around.

The second thing that helped me through this situation was Duke's personnel office. My contact person was amazing. She didn't judge me or the department, and supported me through the entire process. She could have easily said, "You made your own bed, now lie in it!" but she didn't. After the process was explained to me — why I couldn't fire Diana — we began to look for solutions.

The entire process took roughly six months, and during that time (to make things a little more challenging) Diana got pregnant. We spent the entire time looking for positions at Duke where Diana could work and contribute with her limited English skills, all the while knowing that she would have to go on maternity leave shortly after being hired. Simultaneously, I worked closely with personnel to find an excellent replacement for her.

Because of my brother's comments, I began to look at Diana differently. The absolute animosity I had toward her changed to a willingness to help her. I asked her about her family, how she came to the USA, and what the differences in the cultures were. We never became friends, but when she left, I had the feeling she would be better off. I also knew that, although it took six hard months, we handled the situation well.

LETTING GO

Somewhere deep down, we all long to be able to let go of certain situations in our lives. This desire for peace and freedom is understandable — especially if we find ourselves in a relationship in which there seems to be no hope of improvement.

As my HR friend implied, there are situations in which, despite our best efforts, it is not possible to build a bridge to our divas. They are simply not willing to or not capable of cooperating. In these situations it is necessary to let them go.

Depending on what your relationship to your diva is, the process of letting go can look very different. If your encounter with the diva is casual or a one-time incident, you can easily dismiss this person and get on with your life. If, however, this person is a colleague, employee, or your boss, the situation becomes more complicated — doable but more complicated.

Understand that every situation is unique and the guidelines listed below are just that: guidelines. You need to be sensitive to *your* situation and the individuals involved in it. And above all, as you will see below, get help. No matter how helpless a situation may seem and no matter how alone you may feel, there is help available. Be it friends, family, coworkers, your company's HR team, or even an anonymous helpline, there is help available.

STEP: DOCUMENTATION

First and foremost in any conflict situation, it is essential to document everything — both your correspondence and encounters with your diva. This action should not be considered a weapon against your adversary, but as a record to help understand the situation and to better communicate the situation at a later date. This documentation serves as a record of the interactions that you, your team, and anyone else involved in the situation had with the person or persons involved.

In the most ideal situation, you should always document all of your transactions, correspondence, and meetings. This type of diary

Acting on your own without knowing what resources are available to you can be debilitating. Not knowing the rules of your business or organization can defeat your purpose. Know that help is available, and make it your job to find it and get it.

— especially if you began it before tensions developed — will serve you in two very important ways:

1) It is a strong record of the history of your situation which, if kept in actual time (not summarized at a later date), can give deep insights into the challenges in your situation. This will be a strong support if you find it necessary to argue your case against them to a third party.
2) Writing everything down in a diary will help you to organize your own thoughts and feelings, and help you find solutions you otherwise would not have found.

INFORMATION

Acting on your own without knowing what resources are available to you can be debilitating. Not knowing the rules of your business or organization can defeat your purpose. Know that help is available, and make it your job to find it and get it.

Information comes in many forms. In my situation at Duke, the source for most of the information I needed was provided by the personnel office. If you are privileged to be in a company with an excellent personnel or HR office enjoy it! They can be an incredible asset to both you, your team, and your diva. As in my case at Duke, they may not always be the bearer of good news, but — if they are good — they understand their job is to inform, train, and mediate in every way necessary to help you and your team succeed.

Regardless of whether you are an executive, team leader, or a concerned employee, the personnel department is there to assist you. Contact them and ask what your rights and responsibilities are. If you need further support, ask what they offer. Do they offer private, confidential coachings? Do they have mediators who are trained to help in this type of situation?

If you do not have a personnel or HR department in your organization, find information as to what your rights and responsibilities are from other sources. Contact your city hall or chamber of commerce to see what agencies and help lines may exist for your situation, or contact a local lawyer who has specialized in labour law. They will help you find the information and assistance that you need, and usually this information is available for free.

MEDIATION

After you have found out what your rights and responsibilities are, seek someone to help mediate the situation. A professional mediator is a neutral party with no affiliations on either side who will help negotiate a solution. Even if the solution is that one of the people involved has to be fired, having gone through the mediation process will help you and your adversary to better understand each other and to resolve the situation in a respectful manner.

The mediator has the obligation to inform themselves of the situation so they can help the parties reach a mutually acceptable and relevant agreement. There are many different types of mediators. Lawyers, counselors, ministers, or social workers often have some sort of mediation certification in their training. It is important to find someone whose expertise matches your needs and situation.

RELEASE

Last but not least, if you have gone through this book and implemented everything in it, and you are still not able to reach your goals, it is time to consider letting go. With the help of those you have chosen to assist you, decide what, for you, letting go means.

Your situation is unique. Letting go for you may mean something totally different than it would for another person in the exact same situation as you.

Let us take for example an employee who is dissatisfied at work. For one person, letting go may mean finding another position elsewhere, where he will be respected and valued. For another person in the same situation, letting go may mean fighting for his rights. He may decide to sue the company or ask for retribution. Each person and each situation is unique. Get help to decide what is the best option for you and, if relevant, for your team.

EXERCISE:

1) **Begin your journal** *today*! **Even if you don't see the need for it, this step will give you clarity, affirmation, and a sense of accomplishment.**

Last but not least, if you have gone through this book and implemented everything in it, and you are still not able to reach your goals, it is time to consider letting go. With the help of those you have chosen to assist you, decide what, for you, letting go means.

2) Who can help you in your situation? Is there a personnel department available? Make a list of *all* of the people you can think of who would be able to help you in some capacity (coaches, friends, family, labour lawyers, help organizations, etc.):

_____

_____

_____

_____

_____

_____

3) Of all of the people and organizations listed above, who might be able to help you find an appropriate mediator for your situation?

_____

_____

_____

_____

_____

4) And, last but not least, what does "letting go" look like for you?

_____

_____

_____

_____

_____

Postlude

A Personal Note from this "Diva"

In this book we've covered a lot of territory, and you can be proud of yourself for making it all the way through!

If this book has helped you in any way, please go to Amazon and Goodreads and leave a review. This helps others find the book, and it helps us learn more about how we can serve you better in the future.

Also, if you have any questions, comments or ideas about what you have learned or how we can be of further service, please contact me and follow me on social media. The links are below.

Thank you for your trust, for your time, and for your feedback. I wish you all the best, not only in your relationship with your "diva" but in everything you do.

I look forward to hearing from you!

With gratitude and warmest regards,

Laura Baxter

ENDNOTES

Chapter 1:

Information about the surveys I quoted in Chapter 1:

Effectory International is a Dutch company which has specialized in employee engagement. They perform regular international surveys and provide surveys to companies which want to know how engaged their employees are. The results presented here are from the following source:

Erlandsson, Astrid and Penhale Smith, Nik. *The Essential Guide to Driving Employment Engagement in Europe*, Effectory B.V., 2014.

Erlandsson, Astrid and Smith Penhale, Nik. *The Essential Guide to Driving Employment Engagement in Europe*, Broschure by Effectory B.V., 2014.

The survey is available on their website under www.effectory. com.

Gallup continually tracks employee engagement in the USA and abroad. The current number of 32% in the USA is up from 30% in 2012. For more about Gallup Employee Engagement please read this article by Mann and Harter:

Mann, Annamarie and Harter, Jim, "The Worldwide Employee Engagement Crisis," Gallup Business Journal, January 7, 2016.

Web Link: http://www.gallup.com/businessjournal/188033/worldwide-employee-engagement-crisis.aspx?g_source=Business+Journal&g_medium=CardRelatedItems&g_campaign=tiles

For an up-to-date assessment:

http://www.gallup.com/poll/180404/gallup-daily-employee-engagement.aspx

Chapter 2:

Origins of the word "Diva"

Warrack, John and West, Ewan, *The Oxford Dictionary of Opera*. Oxford University Press, 1992. p. 192.

Babiak, Paul and Hare, Robert D., *Snakes in Suits: When Psychopaths Go to Work*, Harper Collins e-Books, 2007.

Television Sitcom: *Happy Days*, created and produced by Garry Marshall, Miller-Milkis Production (1974-1981) and Miller-Milkis-Boyett (1981-1984). The role of Fonzie was played by Henry Winkler, and Richie was played by Ron Howard.

Chapter 3:

Triggers or anchors fall under the category of classical conditioning in behavioral psychology. Psychological research in this area has been going on since the end of the nineteenth century. Early research in this area include Ivan Pavlov's "Pavlov's Dog" experiment and Edwin B. Twitmyer's *A Study of the Knee Jerk* from 1902.

Although most anchors are set subconsciously, it is possible to purposefully (consciously) set them to program a specific desired behavior.

Chapter 5:

Braun, Gesine."Aus Fehlern Lernen: Was Unternehmen besser und schneller macht." *Das Wissen der besten Harvard Business Manager*. Juni 2011.

For more on the History of the 3-M's Post-It® Notes:
Donnelly, Tim. "9 Brilliant Inventions Made by Mistake." *Inc.* 23 August 2012.
Under www.post-it.com/3M/en_US/post-it/contact-us/about-us/

For more on the History of the Scotchgard®:
Moss Kanter, Rosabeth. *Innovation: Breakthrough Thinking at 3M*. Harper Business. 1997.

For more on the History of the Slinky®:
Hunter, Ron and Waddell, Michael E., T*oy Box Leadership: Leadership Lessons from the Toys You Loved as a Child*. Thomas Nelson, 2008, p. 22.
Walsh, Tim. *Timeless Toys: Classic Toys and the Playmakers Who Created Them*. Andrews McMeel Publishing. 2005. pp. 62-65.

For more on the History of the Silly Putty®:
Coupee, Todd. "Nothing Else is Silly Putty!" ToyTales.ca

Chapter 7:

De Shazer, Steve and Dolan, Yvonne. *More than Miracles: The State of the Art of Solution-Focused Brief Therapy*. Haworth Press. 2007.

About SMART goals:

The first known use of the acronym SMART for setting goals was in the November 1981 issue of Management Review by George T. Doran. Since then it has become one of the most commonly used methods to establish goals in organizations. Recently, I encountered the variation SMARTS, where the last "S" stands for sustainability.

Doran, George T. "There's a S.M.A.R.T. way to write management's goals and objectives." Management Review. AMA FORUM. 70 (11). 1981. pp. 35-36.

Chapter 9:

Moss, Richard. *The Mandala of Being: Discovering the Power of Awareness*. New World Library. 2007.

For more information about Torsten Harder and his work: www.myspace.com/torstenharder

Braun, Gesine."Aus Fehlern Lernen: Was Unternehmen besser und schneller macht." *Das Wissen der besten Harvard Business Manager*. Juni 2011.

Burton, Thomas M. "By Learning from Failures, Lilly Keeps Drug Pipeline Full." The Wall Street Journal. April 21, 2004.

"Aus Fehlern Lernen: Warum sich Scheitern lohnt — eine Anleitung in drei Schritten." *Das Wissen der besten Harvard Business Manager*. September 2016.

For information on the history of Post-It Notes, Scotchgard, the Slinky, and Silly Putty, please refer to the endnotes from Chapter 5.

For more on the History of Viagra: http://vardenafilgen.com/history.html

Parasie, Luitgardis and Wetter-Parasie, Jost. *Zum Glück fehlt nur die Krise*. Brunnen. 2009. p. 27.

Chapter 13:

You can find more about the 2005 research by Kathleen Lawler-Row on sleep quality in the following article by Amy Westervelt:

Amy Westervelt, "Forgive to Live: New Research Shows Forgiveness Is Good for the Heart" Good, https://www.good.is/articles/forgive-to-live-new-research-shows-forgiveness-is-good-for-the-heart

The pictures of the polar bears are courtesy of:

Rosing, Norbert. *National Geographic Magazine*. National Geographic Creative. 12/1994 (only two of the pictures were actually published in December 1994)

Chapter 15:

If you would like to find out more about the Biostructure Analysis or find a certified STRUCTOGRAM:registered: trainer near you, visit the STRUCTOGRAM:registered: International website or contact them at:

IBSA Institut für Biostruktur-Analysen AG
Morgartenstrasse 2
CH-6003 Luzern
Tel. +41 41 227 20 10
www.structogram.com

In addition, there are a couple of books available on the subject:

Schirm, Ralf W. and Schoemen, Juergen. *Evolution of Personality*. Structogram. 2003.

China, Ralf and Schoemen, Juergen. *Sei du selbst, sonst geht's dir dreckig*. Börsenmedien. 2017. *(Only available in German)*

Chapter 16:

About the development of the Double Helix:

Wilkens, Maurice *The Third Man of the Double Helix: Autobiography*. Oxford University Press. 2003.

Chapter 17:

The Meta-Position Exercise or Game was first discussed in *The Structure of Magic II* by John Grinder and Richard Bandler. For further interest, Robert Dilts offers an excellent description of the exercise in the *Encyclopedia of NLP*, which can be accessed online under:

http://nlpuniversitypress.com/html2/MdMe24.html

Grinder, John and Bandler, Richard. *The Structure of Magic* II. Science and Behavior Books, Inc. 1976. p. 63ff.

Chapter 19:

I first heard this description of communication by Vera Birkenbihl in one of her many YouTube videos. You can find this video under:

   https://www.youtube.com/watch?v=lrh32N7G3ag

Franklin, Benjamin. *The Private Life of the Late Benjamin Franklin*. London: Printed for J. Parsons 1793.

Franklin, Benjamin. *Autobiography of Benjamin Franklin*. Henry Holt and Company. 1916.

Chapter 20:

Martin, Steve J., Cialdini, Robert B., and Goldstein, Noah. *Yes! 50 Proven Ways to be Persuasive*. Free Press Reprint Edition. 2009.

Research for the mirroring study with tipping can be found in: An Baaren, Rick B., Holland, Rob W.,Steenaert, Bregje, and van Knippenberg, Ad. "Mimicry for Money: Behavioral consequences of imitation." *Journal of Experimental Social Psychology*. pp. 393-398.

Chapter 22:

More Information on the Four-Sides Model can be found in:

Schulz von Thun, Friedemann. *Miteinander reden: Störungen und Klärungen. Psychologie der zwischenmenschlichen Kommunikation*. Rowohlt, Reinbek. 1981.

For more Information on the Logical Levels:

I use the logical levels not only as a communication and change management tool in my work but also as an excellent preparation for presentations (or for any other event, for that matter). By going through each of the levels to see what my client needs at that level, this exercise helps them to be better prepared for whatever may come.

For example, the client lays down a card representing each level. One by one they stand on each level and say what is relevant to level. For the environment they say when and where their presentation will take place. They visualize the presentation and see exactly what they need at the level "Environment." Then they move to the "Behavior" level.

For a thorough history of the logical levels, read this article by Robert Dilts:

http://www.nlpu.com/Articles/LevelsSummary.htm

For a description of the Logical Levels Exercise visit the Encyclopedia of NLP by Robert Dilts:

http://nlpuniversitypress.com/html2/LmLz14.html

About the Author

Laura Baxter, American opera singer and performance coach, has studied the effects of the voice and body on communication and leadership for over 25 years. The focus of her work is presence. She helps her clients master having both a strong inner presence — even in the most difficult situations — and a dynamic, charismatic outer presence. They own the room! In addition to her many stage performances, Laura was the singing voice of Faye Dunaway in the feature film *A Handmaid's Tale*. She was on the faculty at Duke University prior to moving to Germany, and she has been on the faculty of the Friedrich-Alexander-University in Erlangen since 1999. A recipient of the prestigious Louis Sudler Award for the Arts from Emory University, Laura co-authored of several German books including *Die besten Ideen für mehr Humor* ("The Best Ideas for more Humor," GABAL Verlag Top Speakers Edition, 2013) and

Impulse: Präsentieren und Aktivieren ("Impulses: Presentation and Activation," Jünger Verlag, 2016) In her keynote speeches, available in both English and in German, she combines musical theater with leadership topics to create entertaining, inspiring and informative experiences for her audiences.

Laura is the proud mother of two and lives with her husband in Germany.

To find out more about Laura's seminars and keynotes go to her website or follow her on social media:

Website:
www.voice4leadership.com

Social Media:

Facebook:
www.facebook.com/voice4leadership

Twitter:
www.twitter.com/Voice4Leaders
www.twitter.com/_LauraBaxter
www.twitter.com/DealngWithDivas
www.twitter.com/CARMEN_Effect

YouTube:
youtube.com/c/LauraBaxter

LinkedIn:
www.linkedin.com/in/voice4leadership

XING:
www.xing.com/profile/Laura_Baxter

Google+:
google.com/+LauraBaxter

Instagram:
www.instagram.com/voice4leadership

Pinterest:
www.pinterest.com/Voice4Leadership

About Castle Mount Media

"Improving Leadership and Communication
in Healthcare and Education"

Castle Mount Media GmbH & Co. KG is a publishing company located in Erlangen, Germany, which specializes in print and online media dedicated to improving Leadership and Communication especially in the areas of Healthcare and Education. Our mission is to inspire and empower our readers and seminar participants to achieve success through value-based leadership and generative collaboration.

For further information about Castle Mount Media, our online seminars, books, and other products
please visit our website:
www.castlemountmedia.com

More Books from Castle Mount Media:

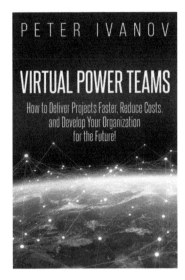

Virtual Power Teams:
How to Deliver Projects Faster, Reduce Costs, and Develop Your
Organization for the Future!
by Peter Ivanov

Globalization and digital transformation have brought about new challenges in leadership and communication. Teams and projects are decentralized, usually crossing international borders, time zones, and cultural boundaries. Leading such teams requires very specific organizational knowledge including how to select qualified experts, which virtual platforms to use, and how to structure and support your team. In this groundbreaking book, Virtual Team Expert Peter Ivanov uses the engaging story of Bernd and his virtual team to show you how to organize, lead, and support your team to be not just a virtual team, but a Virtual Power Team!

English Version:
ISBN 978-3-9818472-3-9
German Version:
ISBN 978-3-8693675-2-1

Next Generation Entrepreneurs:
Live Your Dreams and Create a Better World through Your Business
by Robert B. Dilts

In this first of three volumes, expert author and thought leader Robert Dilts shows both new and experienced entrepreneurs how to connect to their values and mission to create a thriving, value-based organization. With case studies from some of the best leaders of our time, the reader will be inspired and empowered to succeed!

English Version:
ISBN 978-0-9962004-0-0
German Version:
ISBN 978-3-9818472-0-8

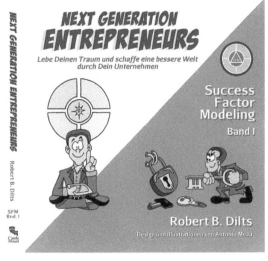

Index

CPSIA information can be obtained
at www.ICGtesting.com
Printed in the USA
JSHW021646021219
2728JS00003B/6